NORTH KINGSTOWN
N K
1898
f L
FREE LIBRARY

THE WORLD OF THE SPIDER

THE WORLD OF THE SPIDER

Adrienne Mason

Sierra Club Books
San Francisco

PAGES II–III

The crab spider (Misumena vatia) *waits motionless, well camouflaged in the center of a flower. The spider uses the lure of pollen to attract and then ambush its unsuspecting prey.*

CHRIS PACKHAM / BBC NATURAL HISTORY UNIT

PAGE IV

For web-weaving spiders such as the shamrock spider (Araneus trifolium), *their almost constant contact with silk is a key to survival. Through their web's silken strands, they receive messages about the arrival of prey, predators, and potential suitors.*

ROBERT MCCAW

The Sierra Club, founded in 1892 by John Muir, has devoted itself to the study and protection of the Earth's scenic and ecological resources—mountains, wetlands, woodlands, wild shores and rivers, deserts and plains. The publishing program of the Sierra Club offers books to the public as a nonprofit educational service in the hope that they may enlarge the public's understanding of the Club's basic concerns. The point of view expressed in each book, however, does not necessarily represent that of the Club. The Sierra Club has some sixty chapters coast to coast, in Canada, Hawaii, and Alaska. For information about how you may participate in its programs to preserve wilderness and the quality of life, please address inquiries to Sierra Club, 85 Second Street, San Francisco, CA 94105.

www.sierraclub.org/books

Originally published in Canada by Greystone Books, a Division of Douglas & McIntyre Ltd., 2323 Quebec Street, Suite 201, Vancouver, B.C. V5T 4S7

LIBRARY OF CONGRESS CATALOGING-IN-PUBLICATION DATA
Mason, Adrienne.
The world of the spider / Adrienne Mason.
p. cm.
Published simultaneously by Greystone Books under title: The nature of spiders.
ISBN 1-57805-044-8
1. Spiders. I. Title.
QL458.4.M38 1999 595.4'4—dc21 99-18378

The quote on page 75 is from *Jaguar of Sweet Laughter: New and Selected Poems* by Diane Ackerman. Copyright © 1991 by Diane Ackerman. Reprinted by permission of Random House, Inc.
Jacket and book design by Val Speidel
Editing by Nancy Flight
Illustration by Donald Gunn
Front jacket photograph by Joe McDonald
Back jacket photograph by Bill Beatty
Printed and bound in Hong Kong by C & C Offset Printing Co., Ltd.

10 9 8 7 6 5 4 3 2 1

CONTENTS

FOR AVA

ACKNOWLEDGMENTS

J. H. Comstock, author of *The Spider Book* (1980) and professor at Cornell University, couldn't have said it better when he commented: "What good are [spiders]? They are damned interesting." Exploring the world of the spider has been a fascinating experience. Not only do spiders spin silk and take to the air without wings, they also have ritualistic courtship and are cunning and inventive in their pursuit of prey. In addition, there is a deep pool of cultural information featuring spiders in stories, superstitions, art, and even dance. What writer could resist? I am grateful to Candace Savage for starting me on this journey by suggesting I write this book.

It is somewhat ironic that I embarked on this project, however, as a spider is the only thing that has ever evoked wild panic in our usually nature-loving household. When my daughter Ava was three I saw firsthand the sheer terror that spiders (albeit plastic ones) can cause. Never before had I seen her scream and shake uncontrollably, and from then on she steered clear of all spiders and anything remotely spidery, plastic or not. (Did you know that some chandeliers look like spider webs when reflected in a spoon?) Nevertheless, we embarked on this project together, and I now have a five-year-old who is a fierce defender of all those creatures that creep the earth on eight legs and who marched out the door last Halloween dressed as a spider.

In his book *The Life of the Spider*, author J.-H. Fabre wrote: "To appoint one's self an

FACING PAGE
The ability to spin silk is the characteristic that sets spiders apart from other creatures. Over half the world's known spiders do not spin webs, however, but may still use silk for everything from swaddling their eggs to luring a mate. The evolution of spider silk has been compared in importance to the evolution of flight in insects, or warm-bloodedness in mammals.
ROBERT MCCAW

inspector of spiders' web, for many years and for long seasons, means joining a not overcrowded profession." Fabre wrote this in 1914, and the same is still true today. Nevertheless, throughout the world, there are hundreds of arachnologists, professional and amateur, tucked away in labs, classrooms, and even their basements, who devote long hours to the study of this most engaging subject. Theirs truly is an uphill battle, as the misinformation and misunderstandings surrounding spiders continue to spread. Appropriately, the Web, the World Wide one, was one of my greatest sources of information and pleasure as I lurked (kind of spiderlike, come to think of it) on arachnology lists with researchers who willingly shared their experience and passion. I am grateful to them for their continuing commitment and research.

Dr. Linda Rayor, Instructor in the Department of Entomology at Cornell University, reviewed the text and assisted me with such incredible enthusiasm and energy that at times I wished I were an undergraduate again and could be whisked away to a lecture in her spider biology class. I'd be in the front row. Her comments were invaluable, and I am most grateful for her assistance. I was delighted that Rick West, one of the world's foremost tarantula experts, also agreed to review the text. His comments and his willingness to answer my calls and e-mail are sincerely appreciated. Dr. Norm Platnick, Dr. Robb Bennett, Dr. Cole Gilbert, and Dr. Neville Winchester also graciously answered my questions. I accept full responsibility for any errors that have crept in since these reviews. Thanks also to Nancy Flight and Candace Savage, who provided excellent editorial advice and brought clarity and polish to the final work.

Finally, as always, thank you to my family and friends, who were forever positive and encouraging and seemed instinctively to know when it was time to whisk the children away. A special thank-you to my father, David, who helped unearth many of the resources I used in my research and who was an enthusiastic supporter of this project. I hope having to track down papers on sexual cannibalism and other such oddities didn't cause him too much embarrassment.

FACING PAGE
The diving water spider (Argyroneta aquatica) *constructs an underwater air-filled "diving-bell" by filling a small, platform-like web with air bubbles carried down from the surface on its hairy abdomen. The spiders eat, mate, and lay their eggs in the diving bell and venture out only to capture small fish, tadpoles, or other pond life.*
HANS PFLETSCHINGER / PETER ARNOLD INC.

SILK AND VENOM:

Part One

THE SECRETS OF SUCCESS

Spiders are found everywhere, and no place is too sacred for their occupation. The walls you lean against, the corners you look into, the books you begin to dust, the grassy lawns over whose soft beds you delight to walk, and even the flowers whose fragrance you enjoy, contain the spiders peculiar to each of these localities.

—N. S. JAMBUNATHAN, *The Habits and Life of a Social Spider* (Stegodyphus sarasinorum *Karsh*), 1905

Wherever you are, there is a spider within a meter of you. The spider may be spinning an architectural marvel of silk, eating its sibling, or sailing through the air on a thread of gossamer. It may be carrying its young on its back, waggling its legs in an elaborate courtship dance, or dining on a meal of liquefied fly. We share our planet with close to 38,000 known species of spiders, and their diversity is remarkable. Whereas approximately 4,000 mammals roam the earth, there are close to 4,400 species of jumping spiders alone.

The consummate predator, spiders are carnivorous hunters, preying on insects, other spiders, and even some vertebrates. There are spiders that hunt or trap or ambush or even steal their food. Once a meal is caught, spiders dispatch their prey using efficient venoms. Mating behavior can include drumming, dancing, and emitting "perfumes."

Spiders are the world's dominant terrestrial carnivores and have successfully

FACING PAGE

The net-casting spider (Dinopsis *sp.*) *casts a postage-stamp-sized net to capture its prey. This spider is also called the ogre-faced spider, in reference to its two huge headlight-type eyes, which are essential for gathering available light during nocturnal hunting forays.*

MICHAEL & PATRICIA FOGDEN

Whereas approximtely 4,000 mammals roam the earth, there are close to 4,400 species of jumping spiders alone.

occupied almost every niche in the world. They are found in habitats as varied as the seashore, the desert, caves, ponds, and mountain peaks. Spiders have been found near the summit of Mt. Everest and in the rigging of ships hundreds of kilometers from shore. They are in our backyards and in our houses. Aside from the ocean and Antarctica, virtually anywhere you care to look, you will find spiders. And their numbers are impressive. British arachnologist W. S. Bristowe calculated that there were 2,265,000 spiders in a single acre of grassy meadow.

What sets spiders apart from other animals is their ability to spin silk. American arachnologist W. J. Gertsch describes silk as being "the most important thing in [a spider's] life, the agent that has largely determined its physical form and dominant place in nature." It has been estimated that all of the silk spun in one day could line the equator and that the amount spun in nine days could extend a silken strand to the moon. Spiders' ingenious and varied use of silk, as well as their use of venom to quell or kill prey, has secured their role as one of nature's most formidable predators.

TO KNOW THE SPIDERS: CLASSIFICATION

Spiders share their classification as arthropods with other jointed-leg creatures such as lobsters, millipedes, scorpions, and insects. Although they are commonly confused with insects, spiders have eight legs instead of six and lack wings and antennae. Spiders and their eight-legged kin, including scorpions, harvestmen, mites, and ticks, belong to the class Arachnida, which takes its name from the spinner Arachne of Greek legend. Ovid tells the story in *Metamorphosis*.

Arachne, a young maiden from Lydia, was renowned for her exquisite weaving. The goddess Minerva had instructed the girl, yet as Arachne's fame grew she became less inclined to honor her teacher. In her vanity, Arachne challenged Minerva to a weaving competition. Although both goddess and mortal wove beautiful tapestries, even Minerva had to admit that Arachne's was superior. Enraged not only at having lost the competition but also by the impertinence of Arachne's portrayal of the gods in less-than-flattering terms, Minerva destroyed Arachne's tapestry and struck her pupil with her spinning shuttle. Humiliated, Arachne attempted to hang herself, but Minerva intervened, rescuing her from one fate and delivering her to another, sprinkling the girl with a noxious herbal remedy. Ovid wrote: "At once all hair fell off, her nose and ears remained not, and her head shrunk rapidly in size, as well as all her body, leaving her diminutive. Her slender fingers gathered to her sides as long thin legs; and all her other parts were fast absorbed in her abdomen—whence she vented a fine thread—and ever since, Arachne, as a spider, weaves her web."

Within the class Arachnida, all spiders belong to the order Araneae. Spiders are further classified into 3 suborders, 2 infraorders, and 106 families on the basis of their structure and behavior. It is not within the scope of this book to cover all currently known spider families; instead, it focuses on the some of the better-known groups of spiders, including those that might reasonably be seen by a curious naturalist. The more common groups are described below. It should also be noted that this book is not intended to be an exhaustive identification guide. A chart summarizing identifying features is included in the appendix; however, those wishing to identify spiders more specifically will need a field guide for their area.

The Survivors (Suborder Mesothelae)

Spiders of the suborder Mesothelae are sometimes referred to as living fossils, since they have a clearly segmented abdomen, a trait that is considered primitive and that no other living spiders share. The one surviving family in this suborder, the Liphistiidae, includes forty species, mostly from Southeast Asia and Japan. Most liphistiid spiders live in caves, where each dwells in a silk-lined retreat

FACING PAGE
Tarantulas such as this Mombasa golden starburst (Pterinochilus murinus) *are recognizable by their large, hairy bodies and small, closely packed eyes. These arachnids are gaining popularity as pets, partly because of their shock value, but also, as Samuel Marshall writes, because "they are denizens of exotic locales and evoke the jungles and deserts of the world in our minds."*
BRIAN KENNEY

capped with a trapdoor. Silken spokes radiate from the trapdoor and alert the spider to approaching prey.

Tarantulas and Their Cousins (Suborder Mygalomorphae)

The suborder Mygalomorphae includes tarantulas (Theraphosidae), and their relatives, trapdoor spiders (Ctenizidae), funnel-web mygalomorphs (Dipluridae), and purse-web spiders (Atypidae).

Mygalomorph spiders can be distinguished from all other spiders by the primitive articulation of their jaws, which lie parallel to one another and strike forward and down. Mygalomorphs are often large bodied, and the tarantulas are relatively hairy. Mygalomorph spiders also breathe using four book lungs, while spiders in the other major suborder, Araneomorphae, use two book lungs and/or tracheae. Book lungs consist of a stack of thin sheets called lamellae that resemble the pages of a book. Air flows in spaces between the blood-filled lamellae, resulting in gas exchange between air and blood.

Most mygalomorphs live a subterranean or terrestrial life. Trapdoor spiders are burrowers that cap their home with a trapdoor; funnel-web mygalomorphs wait in a silken funnel for insects to blunder into the sheet of silk that makes up their web. Purse-web spiders live in a silken tube closed at both ends. Most tarantulas are stay-at-home predators that wait in their silk-lined retreats during the day and partially emerge at night to await passing prey. There are also arboreal species that build their retreats in trees, cliff faces, and road banks. The standard diet of these spiders is insects, but their larger size enables some to capture vertebrate prey, including frogs, snakes, lizards, and mice.

Tarantulas are well-known but widely misunderstood. Contrary to popular belief, most tarantulas do not have venom that is dangerous to humans. Tarantulas are becoming increasingly popular as pets, in part because of their large size,

Spiders in the suborder Mygalomorphae have jaws that lie parallel to one another and strike up and down.
DONALD GUNN

varied coloration, diverse behavior, and exotic reputation. Writer Richard Conniff encapsulates the appeal of owning a tarantula in his essay "Spider Love": "Queen Mary was, in truth, the perfect pet—quiet, furry, at home in an ordinary ten-gallon terrarium. She ate only crickets and never bit the mailman." Although tarantula venom can readily dispatch a cricket, no one has ever died from the bite of a tarantula. (Secondary infection has claimed the life of a few, however.) Nonetheless, cuddling your pet tarantula is not recommended. Irritating barbed hairs of New World tarantulas and impressive fangs large enough to break the skin are tarantula attributes to stay clear of.

The misconceptions surrounding tarantulas actually start with their name, which comes from the village of Taranto, Italy, where, during the Middle Ages, the bite of a spider was blamed for the disease tarantism. Victims of the disease were said to suffer everything from pain, swelling, and nausea to delirium, priapism, and exhibitionism. The popular cure was to perform a frenzied "tarantula dance" for a prolonged period. This dance has survived today as the tarantella.

Curiously, the spider credited with causing tarantism is a large, sedentary wolf spider, *Lycosa tarentula*, whose venom is harmless to humans. Tarantism was well documented during the five hundred years or so that it persisted in Europe, but there is no consensus about the cause of this disease. Some scholars believe that the wrong spider was blamed and that the more venomous European widow spider (*Latrodectus tredecimguttatus*) may have been the real perpetrator. Others propose that because the female victims often dressed in white gowns and tied colored ribbons in their hair—thus mirroring the costume of the ancient priestesses of Bacchus—the "tarantula dance" was used as a pretext for continuing pagan rites and dances, which Christianity had abolished.

Regardless of the identity of the offending spider or the true cause of tarantism, the memory of the spider and its bites persisted, and Europeans took the

THERE ARE MANY STYLES OF WEB—SHEET, TRIANGLE, DOME, AND FUNNEL AMONG THEM—EACH OF WHICH PROVIDES A GOOD CLUE TO THE IDENTITY AND HUNTING METHODS OF THE WEB'S INHABITANT.

name tarantula to North America and elsewhere in the world. In North America, the name was applied to a family of spiders totally unrelated to the European wolf spider, the spiders in the family Theraphosidae. (In this text the commonly used name tarantula will refer to spiders in the family Theraphosidae.)

The True Spiders (Suborder Araneomorphae)

Ninety percent of spiders are classified as "true spiders" and belong to the suborder Araneomorphae. Araneomorph spiders use jaws with opposing fangs that work from side to side like a pair of pliers. As well, they use two book lungs and/or tracheae for breathing. (Mygalomorphs do not have tracheae.)

Among araneomorphs are the orb-weavers, whose striking orb web makes them one of the easier spiders to recognize. But the orb web is just one of the silken marvels engineered by spiders. There are many styles of web—sheet, triangle, dome, and funnel among them—each of which provides a good clue to the identity and hunting methods of the web's inhabitant. Although spiders are sometimes difficult to identify, or even to find, their webs provide one of the best tools for spider family identification. Over 50 percent of the araneomorphs, including wolf, crab, and jumping spiders, do not capture prey with webs, although they may use silk for other purposes.

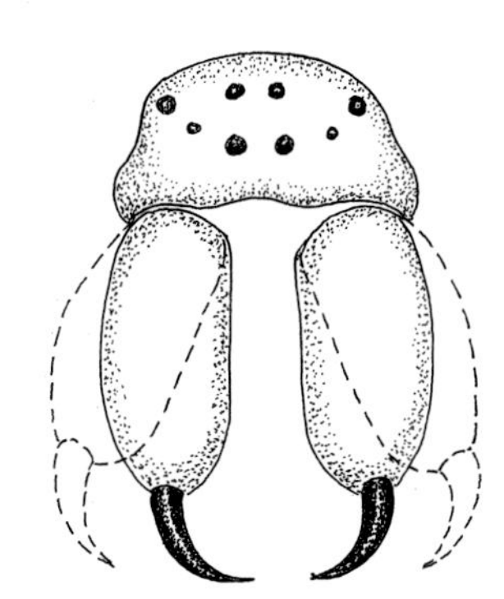

ABOVE
Spiders in the suborder Araneomorphae have jaws that oppose each other and move from side to side.
DONALD GUNN

Orb-Web Spiders (Family Araneidae)

With over 2,600 species in this family, orb-weavers are one of the most successful types of spiders. Their webs are also one of the most recognizable. Arachnologist W. J. Gertsch described this association well when he wrote: "The orb web has long been a symbol of the spider in the mind of man, who sees in its shimmering lightness and intricate, symmetrical design a thing of wonder and beauty."

Orb webs maximize the area for capturing prey while minimizing the amount

The black-and-yellow argiope (Argiope aurantia) *will wrap this unlucky monarch butterfly before biting it and injecting its venom. This method, called offensive wrapping, means there is less danger that the spiders will be harmed by the prey, and the spider will need to spend less time injecting its poison, an important fact if several prey are caught in the web during a short period of time.*

ROBERT MCCAW

FACING PAGE
The grass, or funnel-web, spider (Agelena *sp.*) *dashes out of its tubular retreat when it detects the vibrations of struggling prey on its flat, sheetlike web. The spider then bites its victim and drags it back to its retreat.*
ROBERT MCCAW

of energetically expensive silk used. The silken snares of orb-web spiders are made even more remarkable by the fact that most are created in under an hour and may be rebuilt daily. Just as humans' homes are all slightly different but serve the same basic purpose, there are hundreds of structural variations on the orb-web design. Two other spider families, the Uloboridae and Tetragnathidae, also build orb webs.

One of the more common species of orb-weavers is the garden or cross spider (*Araneus diadematus*), which can be seen sitting in the center of its web throughout Europe and most of North America.

Funnel-Web Spiders (Family Agelenidae)

Even the most suburban lawn is probably home to funnel-web spiders. On cool mornings, their flat webs can be seen suspended like hammocks in the grass, highlighted by dew. If you look closely you can see the narrow, funnel-like tube that leads to the spider's silken retreat. Here the spider sits in ambush mode waiting for an insect to blunder into the web. The flat webs of agelenids can also be seen in the corners of buildings.

The relatively large size, long spinnerets, and conspicuous long legs of the common house spider, *Tegenaria domestica*, can occasionally cause panic in a household as it scuttles across the carpet or finds itself stranded in the bathtub. The hobo spider, *Tegenaria agrestis*, is a European spider that was introduced into the Pacific Northwest of North America. Its venomous bite can be dangerous to people and can result in severely damaged tissues around the bite.

Wolf Spiders (Family Lycosidae)

Wolf spiders are some of the wandering hunters of the spider world and can be seen scurrying over the ground, especially on sunny days, actively hunting for prey. These spiders are quite recognizable not only by their free-living habits (having no

WHEREAS MOST SPIDERS HAVE EIGHT SMALL EYES, WOLF SPIDERS HAVE TWO EYES NOTICEABLY LARGER THAN THE OTHER SIX, AND NOT SURPRISINGLY, WOLF SPIDERS' VISION IS SUPERIOR TO THAT OF MOST SPIDERS.

association with a web) but also by their eye arrangements. Whereas most spiders have eight small eyes, wolf spiders have two eyes noticeably larger than the other six, and not surprisingly, wolf spiders' vision is superior to that of most spiders. Female wolf spiders are easy to recognize by their habits of attaching their egg sac to their spinnerets while hunting, and of carrying their young on their backs.

Many wolf spiders are vagabonds without a permanent retreat, but others live in silk-lined burrows. Most of the three thousand or so species of wolf spiders are a drab brown or grey, a useful disguise for ground dwellers.

Crab Spiders (Family Thomisidae)

Crab spiders' ability to scuttle sideways, along with their enlarged, crablike pair of front legs, gives this family their common name. They are masters at deception and use camouflage and ambush, as well as particularly potent venom, to capture their prey, which can include bees or wasps, meals that most other spiders avoid. Crab spiders do not build webs; instead, they often hide in flowers (thus another common name, flower spiders), blending in beautifully among the stamens, pistils, and petals as they await their prey. Remarkably, some can change color over several days to meld with their background of pink, green, white, or yellow flowers or foliage.

Not all crab spiders exhibit such vibrant colors, however; at the other end of the beauty scale are crab spiders that mimic bird droppings and tree bark. Most of the two thousand or so species are drably dressed in browns and blacks so that they blend in with vegetation or the ground.

Jumping Spiders (Family Salticidae)

Jumping spiders are relatively small, squat spiders with powerful legs. They are most active during the day. As their name suggests, they do leap, often pouncing twenty times their body length or more to seize prey.

FACING PAGE
Wolf spiders are well designed to hunt and pursue prey. Their deadly combination of good vision, subdued coloration, and furtive, roaming habits enables them to use camouflage, speed, and strength to overcome prey.
JOHN R. MACGREGOR/ PETER ARNOLD INC.

FACING PAGE

Their diminutive size and large, inquisitive eyes make jumping spiders one type of spider that even the most hardened arachnophobe might be able to call cute. Jumpers usually stalk prey until they are close enough to pounce.

MICHAEL & PATRICIA FOGDEN

Whereas most spiders have poor vision, jumping spiders have excellent eyesight, which they use to capture prey and court potential mates. One pair of eyes, their large, rather endearing anterior eyes, is among the sharpest in the invertebrate world. These eyes are very visible to the keen observer.

Male jumping spiders are among the most colorful spiders, and many are adorned with iridescent scales, spines, and tufts of bright hair. They use these ornaments to signal one another in elaborate warning displays or during their courtship dance. The female's coloring is more subdued.

MALE JUMPING SPIDERS ARE AMONG THE MOST COLORFUL SPIDERS, AND MANY ARE ADORNED WITH IRIDESCENT SCALES, SPINES, AND TUFTS OF BRIGHT HAIR.

Jumping spiders are one of the most common kinds of spiders in the world, and many species can readily be seen. A species to watch for in the Northern Hemisphere is the zebra spider (*Salticus scenicus*), which is often found sunning itself on exterior walls. *Phidippus audax* is also common and is distinguished by its relatively large size (up to 15 millimeters, or ⅝ inch) and iridescent green jaws.

Six-Eyed Spiders

There are several spider families whose members have only six eyes, the most notable being the Sicariidae, which includes the notorious American brown recluse spider, *Loxosceles reclusa*. The bite of these spiders can be dangerous to humans. Fatal bites are rare, but the venom does destroy tissue around the bite and plastic surgery is often needed. Sicariids live in an untidy web of sticky silk and are fairly common around human habitation. Currently, thirteen species of recluse spiders have been identified in North America, five of which have been implicated in human poisonings.

Spitting spiders (Scytodidae) are the one type of spider that even remotely resembles the comic-book superhero Spiderman in his ability to shoot webbing. Whereas Spiderman can stop his enemies by spraying silk from special spigots on his wrists, spitting spiders capture and immobilize their prey by spraying two streams of sticky "glue" from their fangs. As the spider spits, it rapidly vibrates its jaws, creating two overlapping nets of silk, which pin down the prey. Although most species are tropical, the common spitting spider (*Scytodes thoracica*) is found throughout the world, often in association with humans. This spider can be recognized by its yellow body, flecked with black, and its hump-back appearance, an adaptation necessary to accommodate its enlarged glands, which manufacture both venom and glue. Other features include long, thin legs and six eyes, arranged in three pairs.

Daddy-Longlegs or Cellar Spiders (Family Pholcidae)

Daddy-longlegs spiders have tiny bodies and very long, thin legs. They are sometimes confused with crane flies (a flying insect) and more commonly with another arachnid, the harvestman (order Opiliones). Unlike true spiders, harvestmen have a broad, flat body with a wide attachment between their two body parts, rather than the narrow "waist" of a spider. Harvestmen also have only two eyes.

The pholcid, the long-bodied cellar spider (*Pholcus phalangioides*), is common in homes, where it builds rather untidy webs in corners. When this spider is disturbed it bounces up and down or whirls in circles in a sort of frenzied dance. This tactic makes the spider virtually invisible to predators.

Comb-Footed Spiders (Family Theridiidae)

The name comb-footed refers to a row of bristles on these spiders' last pair of legs, which they use to pull silk from their spinnerets and sling over their prey. Comb-footed spiders spin an irregular, tangled web, sometimes called a cobweb or scaffold web, and most have a distinctive globular abdomen. The comb-footed spiders are one of the largest spider families, with over 2,200 species throughout the world.

Widow spiders have the most recognized name in this group. Their bites

FACING PAGE

Long-bodied cellar spiders (Pholcus phalangioides) *and other spiders in the family Pholcidae are common in caves, cellars, and buildings throughout the world. Along with being efficient predators of insects, they are also successful spider predators, even of species much larger than themselves.*

PREMAPHOTOS

are highly venomous, although a widow bite does not mean certain death to a human. Five species of widow spider are found in North America. The black widows (*Latrodectus mactans* and *Latrodectus hesperus*) are perhaps the most familiar, with their shiny carapace and the red hourglass on the underside of their abdomen. Other widow species also have markings on the abdomen, although not all are in the hourglass shape.

THE COMB-FOOTED SPIDERS ARE ONE OF THE LARGEST SPIDER FAMILIES, WITH OVER 2,200 SPECIES THROUGHOUT THE WORLD.

Sheet-Web Spiders (Family Linyphiidae)

Linyphiids are the most common spiders in temperate regions of the world. Their small, domed sheet webs carpet fields, lawns, and woods and make a striking sight on cool, dewy mornings. The male and female often hang upside-down in the same web, waiting for prey to blunder into the top. After the prey has been caught, the spiders bite it from below and pull it down through the web.

Many sheet-web spiders are tiny, usually measuring less than 2 millimeters (3/32 inch) long, and are commonly referred to as dwarf spiders. Not surprisingly, their small size makes them difficult to see. On warm days, however, when spiders often disperse using a technique called ballooning, dwarf spiders are among the aerialists that "fly" on long, gauzy silk threads. In Britain a common dwarf spider is the money spider, thought to deliver good luck.

FACING PAGE
This stunning widow spider, the malmignatte, or European widow spider (Latrodectus tredecimguttatus), *may have been the spider that caused the disease tarantism. The bite of this spider, like that of all widows, could result in an accelerated heart rate, increased blood pressure, breathing difficulties, and muscle paralysis in humans.*
B. SANTUCCI & G. GUERRIERI/ PANDA PHOTO

Long-Jawed Orb-Weavers (Family Tetragnathidae)

Like araenids, long-jawed orb-weavers spin orb webs, but their design is quite different. After constructing the web, the spider removes its central hub, so the web appears to have a hole in it. The webs of long-jawed orb-weavers are rarely oriented vertically; instead, they are built horizontally or on an angle. Horizontal webs are typically found near water, where they can ensnare aquatic insects emerging from the water.

Situated in a patch of pitcher plants, the web of a funnel-web spider is perfectly placed to intercept insects attracted to these carnivorous plants.

ROBERT MCCAW

The absurdly long jaws of tetragnathids are an easy way to identify members of this family. Jaws this impressive can become a liability during mating, however, so a male tetragnathid is equipped with special spurs on their jaws that hold a female's jaws open and oriented away from his body during copulation.
HELGA LADE/PETER ARNOLD INC.

As their common name suggests, tetragnathids have exceptionally long jaws, which make an ideal clue to identification. Most also have long, slim bodies, and when they are away from their webs, tetragnathids hide by stretching out along a blade of grass, along a twig, or on other vegetation.

The largest web-dwelling spiders are the female orb-weavers *Nephila* sp., which can have a body length of 25 to 50 millimeters (1 to 2 inches). Their webs can be a meter (3 feet) or more wide, and the silk is strong enough to capture larger prey, including birds and bats. The webs are so strong that people in the South Seas used them as fishing nets. Most species of *Nephila* are found in the southern United States and tropical latitudes.

Nursery-Web Spiders (Family Pisauridae)

Nursery-web spiders actively pursue prey and do not build webs. A female nursery-web spider carries her egg sac in her jaws, and just before the young

When away from its web, the common long-jawed orb-weaver (Tetragnatha extensa) *will often stretch out head downwards along a leaf or blade of grass. The spider will sometimes assume this stance while in its web, mimicking the appearance of a blade of grass or a twig that is caught in the web.*

BILL BEATTY

FACING PAGE
Fishing spiders (Dolomedes *sp.*) *often rest on aquatic vegetation but always keep their front legs in contact with the water surface. This position allows them to detect the vibrations of small fish or insects struggling on the water's surface. Their strong jaws and potent venom allow them to overcome prey quickly.*
WOLFGANG BRAUNSTEIN

hatch, she builds a tent and suspends the egg sac inside. The new spiderlings remain in this nursery tent for several days.

Nursery-web spiders resemble wolf spiders in general appearance but are much larger and have different habits. (In addition, whereas wolf spiders have two large main eyes, nursery-web spiders' eyes are all of a similar size.) Although nursery-web spiders actively pursue their prey through vegetation, they can also be seen sitting quietly on vegetation or docks. The fishing spider (*Dolomedes*) is a specialist that sits motionless on the surface of water, waiting for a passing fish or insect. Some *Dolomedes* may even use the ends of their legs as a lure.

Lynx Spiders (Family Oxyopidae)

Lynx spiders are agile, active hunters that use their sharp eyesight to find and pursue prey. They often travel in vegetation, and many are green, affording them protective camouflage. Many lynx spiders are recognizable by the spines on their legs and their slim abdomens, which taper to a point. These spiders also have a unique eye arrangement, with six larger eyes forming a hexagon and two smaller eyes below. Most lynx spiders are tropical, although a few species are found in North America and Europe.

HAIRY LEGS AND ALL: A TOUR OF THE SPIDER

The appearance and demeanor of spiders is certainly enough to capture the attention of both the fearful and the fascinated—eight eyes (in most species), sharp fangs, furry bodies, furtive habits, hairy legs, and more. Love them or loathe them, they don't go unnoticed.

Spiders have two body parts: the cephalothorax is joined by a narrow "waist," or pedicel, to the abdomen. The cephalothorax is the site of more active pursuits—locomotion, feeding, and sensory perception—and accordingly houses the brain, poison glands, stomach, and eyes. It is also the point of attachment for the spider's chelicerae (jaws), palps, and eight jointed legs. The softer, rounder abdomen is the site for more passive tasks and contains the heart, digestive tract, reproductive organs, respiratory tracheae or book lungs, and silk glands. The delicate, wasplike pedicel connects the aorta, intestine, and nerve cord and some muscles between the two sections.

The Exoskeleton

In the 1958 film *Tarantula*, Clint Eastwood makes a brief appearance as an air force pilot given the task of napalming a 30-meter-tall (100-foot-tall) cattle-eating tarantula that's ravaging the Arizona desert. Hollywood aside, the largest known spider is the goliath birdeater (*Theraphosa blondi*), a tarantula with legs that could span a small pizza. But most spiders are less than 2.5 centimeters (1 inch) long.

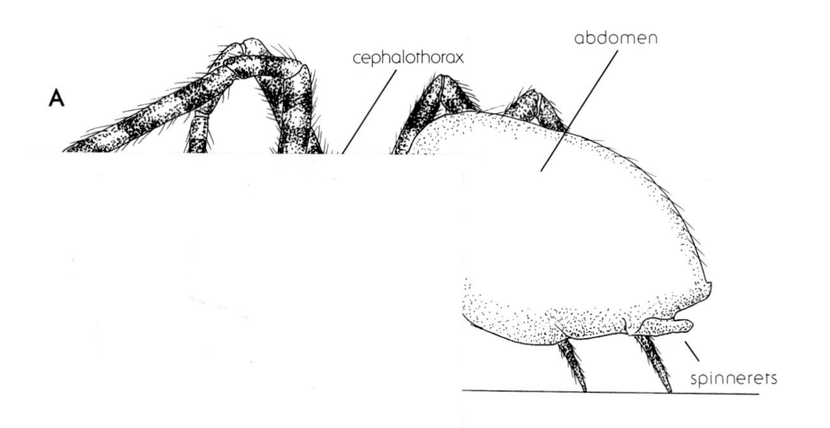

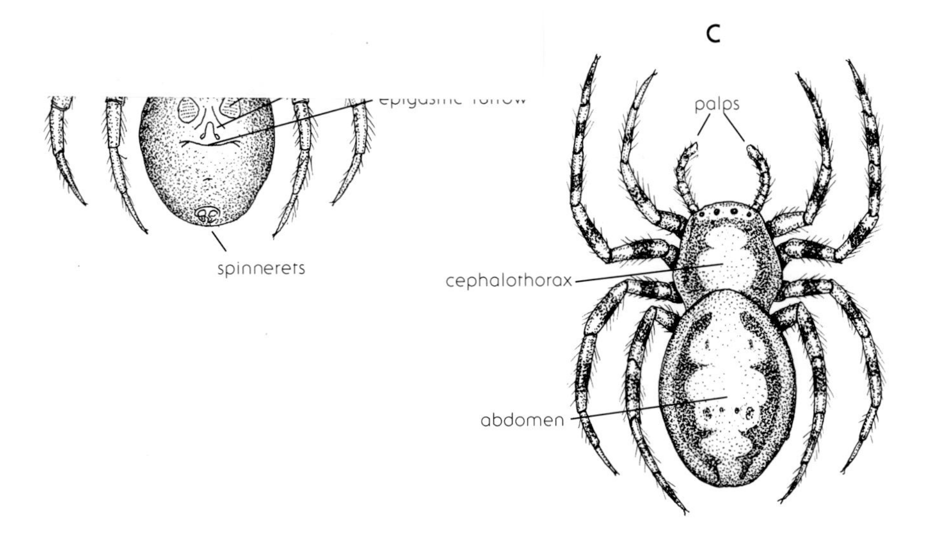

Generalized spider: (A) side view, (B) ventral view, (C) dorsal view.
DONALD GUNN

Spiders and other arthropods are restricted in size by their hard body covering, the exoskeleton.

The exoskeleton is made of a stiff material that has limited flexibility and must be shed periodically for a spider to grow. Since periodic molting taxes spiders' energy and creating a new exoskeleton strains their limited resources, the sheer frequency of the molts that would be required for spiders to attain Hollywood proportions makes this size a biological impossibility.

Much like a suit of armor, the exoskeleton is a perfect compromise between the need to support and protect delicate internal organs and the need to be flexible enough for movement. In addition, the structure must be strong, waterproof, and light. To ensure that it can fulfill its varied functions, the exoskeleton is made of four distinct layers, stacked in a strong, natural laminate. Where spiders need the most protection, such as in the cephalothorax, all four layers are present. In the parts of the exoskeleton where greater flexibility is required—the joints and the abdomen (which must be able to expand to accommodate the female's eggs)—only the more flexible cuticle layers are present.

Effective as it is for protection, an exoskeleton eventually becomes a straitjacket for a growing spider. So to make space for new growth, spiders go through a periodic, hormone-induced molt, or ecdysis (Greek for "getting out"), in which the exoskeleton is shed and replaced by a new one. Rather than growing until the skeleton is bursting at the seams, spiders do most of their growing immediately after shedding the old skeleton, when the new exoskeleton is still soft and pliable.

Although this recurrent striptease gives spiders room to grow, their temporarily soft body makes them vulnerable. To be less exposed to predators, before molting most spiders suspend themselves from a strand of silk; tarantulas and some other mygalomorphs retreat to their burrows.

Understandably, new tarantula owners might be startled if they found their

To protect their temporarily soft body after a molt, most spiders, including this tetragnathid (Nephila inaurata madagascariensis), *hang from a silken thread during and after molting.*
WOLFGANG BRAUNSTEIN

FACING PAGE
Tarantulas and other types of wandering spiders usually lie on their backs to molt. The molting mat and shed exoskeleton of this orange baboon spider (Pterinochilus murinus) *are visible here.*
BRIAN KENNEY

pet lying on its back with its feet in the air, but usually this just means the spider is preparing to be retrofitted with a new exoskeleton. Before becoming supine, however, spiders display other telltale signs of the impending molt, including a lack of interest in food—all spiders fast before molting—and generally lethargic behavior. Most tarantulas also busily spin a thick silk mat, the bed they will lie on as they molt. Some arboreal tarantulas spin a silk hammock in preparation for molting.

While a spider rests, its new exoskeleton forms beneath the old one. During this time some of the old exoskeleton is reabsorbed into the spider's body to minimize the amount of new building material that needs to be created. A special molting fluid is produced underneath the old skeleton and creates a space between the old and new skeleton. When the new skeleton is completed, the fluid is reabsorbed, leaving an air-filled gap that allows the two skeletons to easily separate.

To start the molt, the heart rate of the spider increases and pumps more hemolymph (a spider's equivalent of blood) into the cephalothorax. This flush of fluid causes the weight of the cephalothorax to increase by about 80 percent, while the weight of the abdomen is reduced by 30 percent. The pressure of the fluid causes the cephalothorax to split along the sides, and eventually the old carapace, or protective back, hinges away, like the lid of a can, and the "new" spider emerges. Still hanging from a thread or sheltered in its burrow, the spider now repeatedly bends and stretches its legs to ensure supple joints.

Depending on the species, most spiders go through three to ten molts in their lifetimes. With their final molt, they achieve sexual maturity and assume adult characteristics. Before this time, aside from differences in size (the females are usually larger), it is often difficult to tell males and females apart. The final molt reveals the swellings on the tips of the male's palps, which are used for mating. Most spiders live for only one year, perhaps two, and do not molt as adults. Some tarantulas are an exception, however; females, which often live ten to

EFFECTIVE AS IT IS FOR PROTECTION, AN EXOSKELETON EVENTUALLY BECOMES A STRAITJACKET FOR A GROWING SPIDER.

twenty years, periodically molt and replace worn or missing appendages and the barbed urticating hairs that are used in defense.

The Eyes

Although spiders have multiple eyes, most species have poor vision. The majority of spiders rely almost entirely on tactile and chemical cues to perceive their world and use their limited vision to detect movements and changes in light. Except in a few species, spider vision has been poorly studied.

Most spiders have eight eyes; spitting spiders and some daddy-longlegs spiders have only six. A few species have four or even two eyes. Some cave-dwelling spiders appear to have lost their eyes altogether as they evolved, although there is some question as to whether these eyes are present but simply inactive. Spider eyes are usually arranged in two transverse rows of four along the front margin of the cephalothorax, but in some species the eyes are found in three rows. The size, number, and arrangement of eyes are important clues for taxonomists who classify and identify spiders.

THE SIZE, NUMBER, AND ARRANGEMENT OF EYES ARE IMPORTANT CLUES FOR TAXONOMISTS WHO CLASSIFY AND IDENTIFY SPIDERS.

Most spiders have two types of eyes, each serving a different function. The center front pair of eyes, or main eyes, has direct retinas made of light-sensitive cells that point towards incoming light. These eyes provide spiders with the most acute image of their surroundings, although this “image” is negligible in many species. Spiders’ secondary eyes have indirect retinas, with light-sensitive cells that point away from the light, much as they do in the human eye. Secondary eyes are often lined with a tapetum, a light-sensitive structure that helps improve spiders’ vision in low light. The tapetum is what gives spiders and other creatures reflective eyes at night. Secondary eyes detect light and motion, which prompt spiders to turn towards the object so that they can focus in on it with their main eyes.

Active hunters—the crab, wolf, and jumping spiders—have a good visual sense. They use vision not only to capture prey but also to recognize potential partners during courtship. Their visual acuity is due to the greater number of receptors in their eyes than in the eyes of more sedentary web-dwelling spiders.

Jumping spiders have the premier eyes in the spider world, and vision is their strongest sense. (Not surprisingly, jumping spider eyes are the most studied and best understood.) Their main eyes act as tiny telephoto lenses, with a small field of vision at high resolution. As a result, they have good sight at a greater distance than other species do. The secondary eyes give them a greater field of view, and the outer eyes of the front row provide binocular vision. This combination gives these tiny spiders the ability to judge distances, which comes in handy when pouncing on prey.

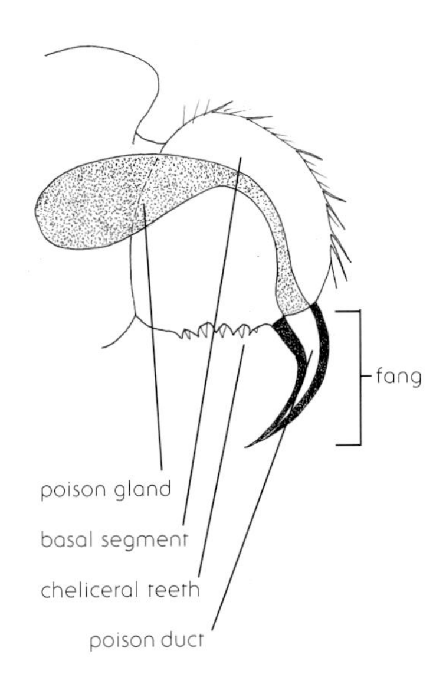

The Jaws

After finishing his meal of roasted tarantula with a family of Piaroa Indians from Venezuela, tarantula expert Rick West followed the lead of his hosts and used one of the tarantula's 2-centimeter-long (¾-inch-long) fangs to pick the exoskeleton out of his teeth. An unconventional use of this "tool" for sure, but the jaws, or chelicerae, serve a multitude of uses for the spider also. They are something like a spider's equivalent of a Swiss Army knife.

Spider chelicerae have two parts, a stout basal segment and a movable articulated fang. At the tip of the fang is a small opening that delivers the venom to prey. This opening connects to the spider's venom glands, which, depending on their size, may be contained within the basal segment of the chelicerae or extend back into the head.

Besides being used for defense or to subdue prey, chelicerae are used as pliers; they can be considered the equivalent of spider hands. Burrowing spiders,

ABOVE

With a few exceptions, spiders use potent and efficient venom to subdue and kill their prey. These deadly concoctions are delivered through an opening at the tip of the fang. When not in use, fangs rest in a groove in the basal segment.

DONALD GUNN

The active and agile green lynx spider (Peucetia viridans) *is often seen running and leaping through vegetation in pursuit of prey. This spider can spit venom at aggressors from as far away as 20 centimeters (8 inches).*
JAMES ROBINSON

including tarantulas, use their chelicerae to dig their burrows. Nursery-web spiders, spitting spiders, tarantulas, and many other spiders carry their egg sacs in their chelicerae. In spiders that masticate their food before consuming it, the underside of the basal segment of the chelicerae is covered in tiny teeth, which aid in breaking down prey.

The Palps

Just behind the chelicerae are the spider's jointed palps. Although they resemble a pair of legs, palps are shorter and have one less segment (palps have 6 segments). Like the chelicerae, palps are a multi-tasking appendage and are used widely in feeding and sex and for digging.

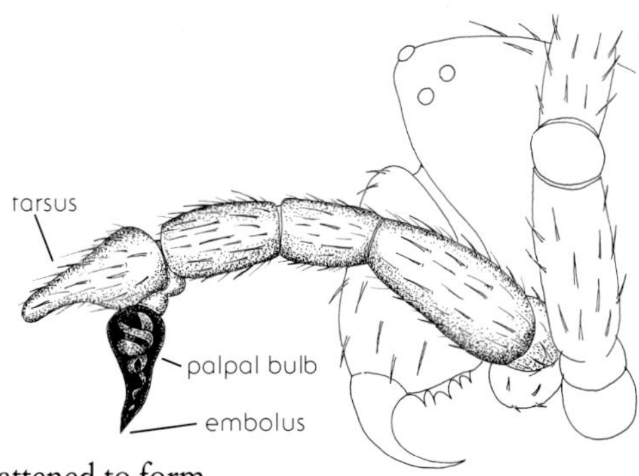

The segment of the palps closest to the head is expanded and flattened to form an accessory jaw called the maxilla. This jaw frames the mouth, and its serrated edges are used to manipulate and break up food. The maxilla's inner edge has a mustache-like fringe of hair that acts as a filter and also channels the liquefied food towards the spider's mouth.

In a male spider, the last segment of the palps is used to transfer sperm to the female. After the final molt, the last segment of each palp becomes enlarged and knoblike, somewhat like a boxing glove. In many species palps are waved and displayed during courtship and, like mini-semaphore flags, relay a message to the female.

The Legs

> *"You have awfully hairy legs, Charlotte," said Wilbur, as the spider busily worked at her task.*
>
> *"My legs are hairy for a good reason," replied Charlotte. "Furthermore, each leg of mine has seven sections—the coxa, the trochanter, the femur, the patella, the tibia, the metatarsus, and the tarsus."*
>
> —E. B. WHITE, *Charlotte's Web*

Charlotte knew her anatomy well, although she didn't elaborate on the detailing on the tip of her tarsus. Web-weaving spiders also have a smooth middle hook and two claws with serrated edges that are used in constructing webs. The middle hook manipulates silk threads by folding down over the strands, forcing them to snag on the barbed hairs around the claws. To release the silk, the spider lifts the hook and the elastic thread springs back out of its clasp.

Free-roaming hunting spiders such as tarantulas, wolf spiders, and jumping

ABOVE
Male palps are used to transfer sperm from the male to the female. The inflated palpal bulb functions somewhat like an eyedropper, first sucking up sperm from the male's abdomen or sperm web and then delivering it to the female.
DONALD GUNN

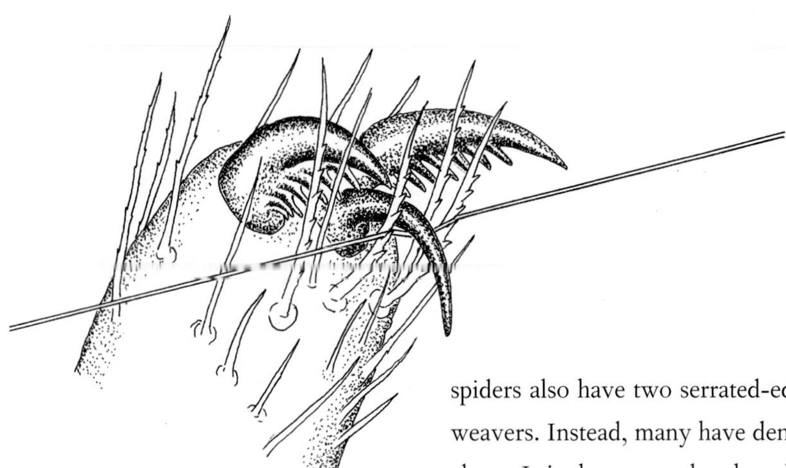

spiders also have two serrated-edged claws but lack the middle hook of the web weavers. Instead, many have dense tufts of hair, called scopulae, surrounding the claws. It is these scopulae that allow some spiders to walk on smooth walls and even windowpanes. How they are able to do this becomes clearer when you look at the fine detailing of the scopula hairs. The underside of each hair splits into thousands of fine end-feet, giving each hair a tufted, brushlike appearance. End-feet dramatically increase the number of contact points on each scopula hair. A crab spider, for instance, with 30 scopula hairs on each foot, and 500 to 1,000 end-feet on each scopula hair, can have 160,000 contact points. These end-feet do not function with suction, however; rather, simple forces of physical adhesion enhance their grip.

As Charlotte noted to her friend Wilbur, her legs are hairy for a good reason. Legs are the primary sensory organ for most spiders, and they are involved in not just one, but three, and possibly four, methods of perceiving their environment.

Spiders are one of the few animals that use their legs to taste their food. On the tip of the palps and legs are contact chemoreceptors, specially adapted hollow hairs that allow spiders to taste by touch. An adult spider can have over a thousand of these chemo-sensitive hairs. Spiders usually handle potential prey before eating it, and lab studies have shown that they readily accept and eat freshly killed flies, whereas they quickly discard old, dead flies. Spiders also often drop certain insects after touching and "tasting" them with their legs; this unusual method of sensory perception probably alerts them to the unpleasant taste of certain insects.

Spiders also "hear" with their legs, using triply innervated hairs on their legs and their bodies to detect vibrations. Some of the hairs are tactile, or sensory, hairs; spiders react when the hairs are touched. Other hairs, the trichobothria, are less numerous than tactile hairs and are usually found in clusters on the legs.

Trichobothria are "touch-at-a-distance" receptors and are so sensitive that

ABOVE

To ensure a firm grip on silk threads, web-weaving spiders use a combination of two serrated comblike claws and an articulated, smooth central hook. This hook pushes the silken lines against barbed hairs that surround the claws, causing them to snag and hold.

DONALD GUNN

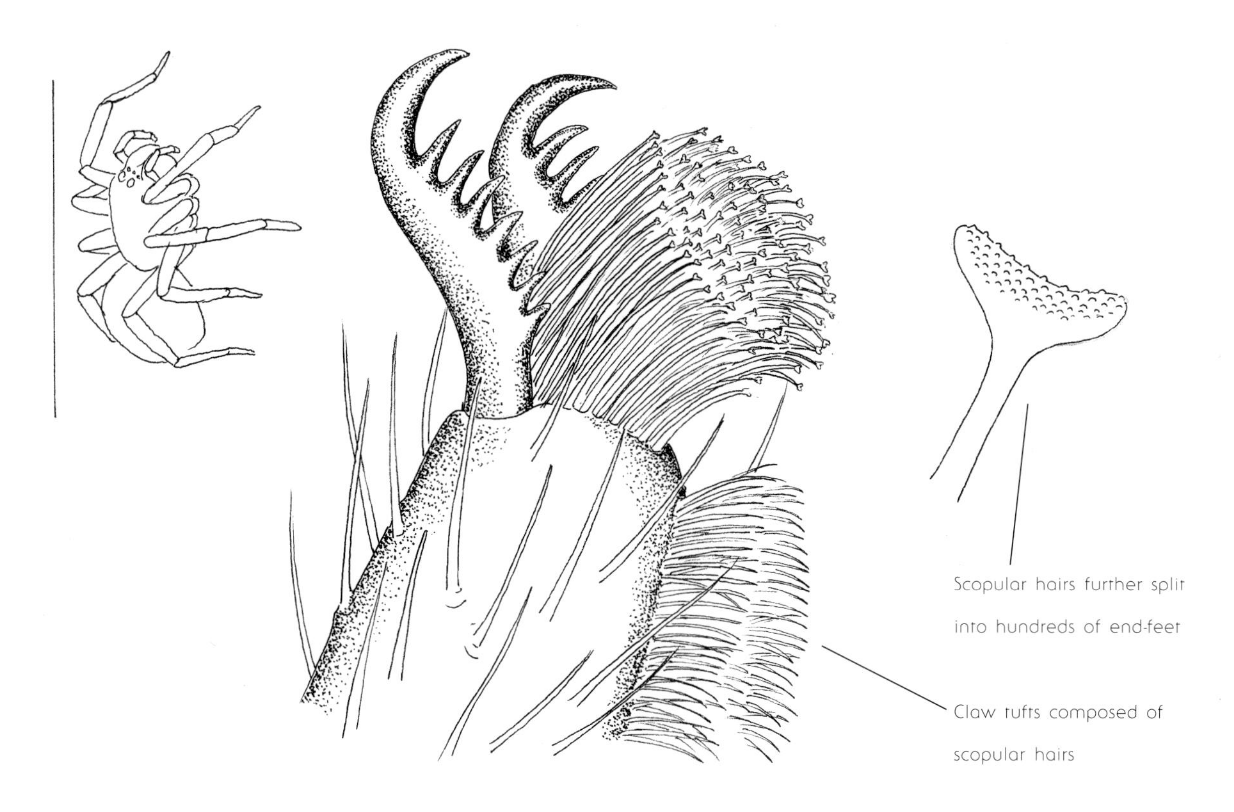

ABOVE

Free-roaming spiders have only two tarsal claws. They use brushlike tufts of hair, called scopulae, to allow them to walk on a variety of surfaces, including those that are smooth and vertical. The ventral surface of each of these scopula hairs splits into hundreds or even thousands of fine end-feet, which facilitate adhesion.

DONALD GUNN

even the slightest air current of 1 millimeter (1/16 inch) a second can make the hair quiver. This degree of sensitivity is enough to detect the air vibrations from a flying insect, and one study showed that a totally blinded spider could locate a buzzing fly 30 centimeters (1 foot) away. In further studies, however, when all of the trichobothria were removed, the spider could still orient to the prey. This finding signaled to researchers that there was yet another sensory organ involved in detecting movement.

Trichobothria are, in fact, early-warning detectors, and other sensory tools—mechanical vibration receptors called slit sensilla—are used to further orient the spider to the vibrations. Slit sensilla are tiny openings in the exoskeleton. A spider can have up to three thousand slit sensilla scattered over its body surface, although most are found in the legs. When there is movement nearby—of a predator, prey, or potential mate—the vibrations travel through the substrate and into the spider's exoskeleton. The vibrations cause the exoskeleton to flex, and these flexions are intercepted and interpreted by nerves in the slit sensilla, telling the spider the size and location of the movement and enabling it to decide whether to attack or flee.

Whereas taste requires direct contact with a substance, smell can occur at a distance via airborne, volatile chemicals. Spiders use smell during courtship and to recognize prey or predators. Smell can elicit a strong reaction, and males often go through elaborate courtship rituals in front of a spot where a female *used* to be in response to her smell. Although it is agreed that spiders have a sense of smell, how they use it is still under debate. Small openings in the legs, the tarsal organs, were originally thought to be the primary site for olfaction, but these openings have since been shown to react more to humidity and temperature than to odor. Thus, the question of where spiders actually perceive smell remains unsolved, although the legs are still a most likely answer.

Silk Glands and Spinnerets

> *Silk is the warp and woof of the spider's life.*
>
> —THEODORE H. SAVORY, *Spiders, Men and Scorpions*

Spiders are set apart from all other animals by their universal ability to spin silk. Although some insects can produce silk, the best-known being the silkworm, spiders are nature's silk specialists, the ultimate spinners. Throughout their lives, spiders are in almost constant contact with silk—from the silk cocoon they were swaddled in as eggs to the silken snares they use to capture food to the scent-laden silk lines used as sexual lures.

The most visible features on the spider's abdomen are the finger-shaped spinnerets, the external openings of the silk glands. Most spiders have three pairs of spinnerets that are covered in tiny spigots that extrude the silk. In total, a spider

This orb-weaver (Araneus) *exudes a strand of silk from its spinnerets. Its silken lines are a concoction of several types of liquid silk extruded from hundreds of tiny spigots on each of the spider's six spinnerets.*
BILL BEATTY

can have thirteen hundred spigots on its spinnerets. Some spiders have an additional spinning organ called the cribellum, a small plate in front of the spinnerets that is paved with up to forty thousand minute spigots. The cribellum produces the extremely fine "hackle-band" or catching silk used by some spiders.

The secret of silk, a material of exceptional strength and elasticity, is a subject under much scrutiny these days. Being able to mimic such an incredible fiber—particularly the spider's dragline silk, which is stronger than steel wire of the same diameter and as flexible as a bungee cord—is the Holy Grail of scientists looking for current applications of natural materials. As Janine Benyus states in her book *Biomimicry*, spider silk is "a 380-million-year-old fiber with a twenty-first century future." The ideas for how to use this fiber—if it could be synthetically produced in quantity—run the gamut from artificial ligaments to parachutes to bulletproof vests.

Spiders don't make just one type of silk, however; most make three or four,

THROUGHOUT THEIR LIVES, SPIDERS ARE IN ALMOST CONSTANT CONTACT WITH SILK—FROM THE SILK COCOON THEY WERE SWADDLED IN AS EGGS TO THE SILKEN SNARES THEY USE TO CAPTURE FOOD TO THE SCENT-LADEN SILK LINES USED AS SEXUAL LURES.

FACING PAGE
The orb web of the black-and-yellow garden spider (Argiope aurantia) *is adorned with a fuzzy "hackle-band" silk, which is produced by the spider's spigot-studded spinning organ, called the cribellum.*
BRIAN KENNEY

and orb-weavers can make seven. Each type of silk is created in its own gland and has its own particular set of properties, depending on its final use. Dragline silk, for instance, is used for the "frame" in orb webs and is trailed behind most spiders as a sort of safety line. It has been calculated that a strand of dragline silk could stretch through the air 80 kilometers (50 miles) before snapping under its own weight.

Liquid silk is a protein soup with both rigid microscopic crystals and flexible strands of protein. As silk is extruded through the spigots, the protein molecules are forced to line up parallel to one another, resulting in a solid, rodlike thread. Valves on the spigots control the amount of silk leaving the gland and the diameter of the thread. Most silk threads have a diameter of 1 to 2 microns, although the extremely fine threads of hackle-band silk can be 0.01 micron to 0.02 micron in diameter. For comparison, a blond human hair is 100 microns in diameter.

Although silk threads appear to be a single fiber, they are actually composed of multiple strands. The simplest fiber would be two strands of the same type of silk extruded from two different spigots. Other threads are composites, created from different types of silk. The spiral threads in an orb-weaver's web, for instance, are made from a double strand of ground line extruded from one gland, coated in a thin film of sticky silk, which originates in another gland. As the spider slowly spins this line, it periodically jerks on the line, causing the sticky fluid to form beadlike globules along the thread.

The complexity and variety of spider silk and the myriad uses for it could fill several books, and indeed they have. But in *Charlotte's Web* E. B. White sums up the wonder of spiders' engineering prowess well:

> "What's so miraculous about a spider's web?" said Mrs. Arable. "I don't see why you say a web is a miracle—it's just a web."
> "Ever try to spin one?" asked Dr. Dorian.

Perhaps the most recognizable symbol of the spider, the orb web varies widely in design and style from species to species. Web construction and specific design seem to be innate, as spiderlings are able to spin a perfect web within days of hatching.

ROBERT MCCAW

THE LIFE OF A SPIDER: *Part Two* FROM EGG TO THE AIR

In view of his superfluous nature in any role save that of providing the fertilising sperm for the eggs, [the male spider] has become something of a specialist for that single role, which often makes the severest demands upon both his skill and courage.

—ROD PRESTON-MAFHAM AND KEN PRESTON-MAFHAM, *Spiders of the World*

DANCING, DRUMMING, AND DEATH: SPIDER SEX

Something about the sex life of spiders makes even the most ardent scientists venture into the normally taboo realm of anthropomorphism. There's talk of love dances and tickles, caresses and serenades, bondage and rape. As American arachnologist W. J. Gertsch wrote, "The bringing together of the sex cells is accomplished by these arachnids in a manner so extraordinary that the various strange details almost transcend belief." Indeed, spider sex is enticing enough to bring out the voyeur in all of us.

The early days of a spider's life are celibate and are devoted solely to the pursuit and capture of food. After the final molt, when a spider becomes sexually mature and the male's palps develop their thickened, mittenlike shape, the male leaves his web or retreat and begins his search for a receptive female.

Before mating, however, the male's first task is to transfer semen from his

FACING PAGE
The dramatically outsized male St. Andrew's cross spider (Argiope aetherea) *entices a female out of her web and onto a mating thread by plucking a rhythmic message.*
WOLFGANG BRAUNSTEIN

BECAUSE SPIDERS ARE EFFICIENT PREDATORS, BEING RECOGNIZED AS A PARAMOUR AND NOT PREY IS CRITICAL FOR A MALE SPIDER.

testes to his palps, since nature has not provided a direct connection between the two. The challenge is to devise a technique where sperm can be transferred without drying out. Many insects and other arachnids, including scorpions, transfer sperm in neat packages called spermatophores. But the male spider has developed another technique to deliver its sperm to the female.

First the male spider spins a small sperm web, which can vary from a single silk thread to a small triangular web, not much larger than the eraser on the end of a pencil. Next he presses his genital opening against the sperm web until a drop of sperm is deposited on the web. He then moves to the underside of the sperm web and reaches his palps up and around its edge. He alternately dips an extension of his palp, called the embolus, into the drop of sperm and draws it into a reservoir where the sperm will be stored until it is delivered to the female.

During mating the male's embolus is inserted into the female external genital opening, called the epigynum. To ensure that the male mates with a female of the same species, both structures match, much like a lock and key. A long, convoluted epigynum, for instance, will usually require a correspondingly long and coiled embolus.

Courtship

Mating can be a dangerous business. Because spiders are efficient predators, being recognized as a paramour and not prey is critical for a male spider. His challenge is an impressive one. Not only must he find a female, he must convince her to put aside her natural predatory instincts and solitary tendencies long enough to permit copulation. Finally, if all goes well, they will mate and he'll escape before being eaten. Sexual cannibalism before, during, or after sex is not a given for all spiders; however, for many species the possibility that a male will be eaten by a rapacious female is a very real hazard of courtship.

To help ensure successful mating, spiders have evolved elaborate courtship rituals. Each species has its own repertoire and unique code, depending on its habits and the strength of various senses. Courtship can vary from almost none —a sort of pounce-and-mate technique—to elaborate dances, web plucking, or drumming.

The male's first task is to locate a female of the right species. Since spiders' vision is typically poor, most males initially home in on females using smell or touch. Many spiders locate their mates using pheromones, chemical attractants released by females shortly after their last molt. Males can find females by following their pheromone-scented silk, a spider's equivalent to a perfume-drenched love letter.

Both pheromones and vision trigger courtship in male wolf spiders, but the attractive power of pheromones can sometimes supersede the role of sight. For example, in laboratory experiments confused males have performed their elaborate courtship dance in front of a female's severed leg or to a piece of blotting paper recently vacated by a female.

After he has found a potential mate, the male needs to signal his amorous intentions. Tarantulas, among other types of spiders, do a sort of courtship dance. Although the routine varies among species, the dance usually includes full-body jiggles and leg and palpal drumming. A receptive female tarantula may look a little imposing as she rises on her hind legs and flashes her jaws, but the male is ready. As he advances, he secures her fangs on special leg spurs, designed specifically for this purpose. The spurs (which some tarantulas lack) are thought to help position the female for mating and to hold the female's chelicerae open so that she cannot bite the male.

Wolf spiders also perform an elaborate courtship dance, with steps that would make a choreographer proud. Upon seeing a female, the male stops abruptly and

FACING PAGE *The male nursery-web spider* (Pisaura mirabilis) *presents a gift—a fly wrapped in silk—to a female as a precursor to mating. If she is receptive, she will seize the gift and begin to feed. While the female is preoccupied with her meal, the male will slip under her abdomen and begin to copulate.* PREMAPHOTOS / BBC NATURAL HISTORY UNIT

rises high on his hind legs. He stretches out his palps, one upwards at a 45-degree angle and the other downwards at the same angle. In this somewhat awkward position, he jerkily walks forward while quivering his palps, legs, and abdomen. As he dances, he occasionally reverses the position of his palps or rapidly vibrates his front legs. A female wolf spider will often respond to the male's dance with her own ballet, replete with postures, body quivers, and palp or leg waving.

Probably because wolf spiders are often found in leaf litter or other habitats where visibility is limited, some have added sound to their mating behavior. They produce loud whirring noises (reported to be like a those of a motorcycle revving up) by dragging a spur on the cuticle over a file on the palp. Sound cues may also be used during courtship at night.

COURTSHIP CAN VARY FROM ALMOST NONE—A SORT OF POUNCE-AND-MATE TECHNIQUE—TO ELABORATE DANCES, WEB PLUCKING, OR DRUMMING.

Jumping spiders are among the most colorful and behaviorally complex spiders, and it is not surprising that their courtship rituals are filled with a wide repertoire of mating dances. Unlike most species of spider, jumping spider species rely primarily on visual courtship cues. Many have exquisite ornamentation to further accent their courtship dances. Jumping spiders are often brightly colored, and some even have iridescent green chelicerae. Depending on the species, their front legs—an important accessory in their mating dance—may have fringes of long hairs, scales, or even spines. The jumping spider's dance begins when he raises these long front legs into a vertical position, much like the football signal for a touchdown. Next he moves forward, often in a zigzag pattern—three steps to one side, three to the other—all the while shimmying his body and wagging his fringed and decorated palps.

A receptive female jumping spider will often respond by vibrating her palps; sometimes she may even imitate the male's courtship routine. She may also wait quietly in a crouching position until the male approaches her to copulate.

The European nursery-web spider (*Pisaura mirabilis*) uses bribery, in the form of dinner, to entice his mate. He first catches a fly and wraps it in silk. Then he marches off, parcel firmly clenched in his jaw, in search of a potential mate. When he finds a female, he lowers his abdomen and raises his gift towards her, like a worshipper making an offering at an altar. If she approaches him, he leans over backwards, tempting her with the fly. As she reaches up to grasp it, he quickly swivels around under her. While she's busy eating her snack, he mates with her. The fly-as-peace-offering is a crucial step in the courtship of this species. When giftless males were placed in a cage with a female, she ate them. No gift, no sex.

Finding prospective mates is usually not a problem for male web-weaving spiders, which locate females by following their scented silk. Males can also use the silk as a mechanical cue, since they've been known to follow old draglines that have long ago lost their scent. If a male encounters the middle of the dragline, however, he has a dilemma. Which direction should he take to find his mate? To find out, the male travels along the line looking for the nearest attachment disk, a point where the line was anchored to the ground. Once there, he plucks the silk thread on either side of the disk with his palps to determine its tautness (the tighter end probably leads to her web) and then sets off in the right direction.

After the male orb-weaver has found a female, though, things can get a little tense. Until now, she has been focused on killing anything that enters her web. To signal to her, the male uses the web as a harp; he plucks and tweaks the web in a rhythmic pattern. The regular cadence of his message delivers a different "feel" to the female than a struggling insect would. Female web-building spiders often respond by plucking a pattern on the web that corresponds to the male's pattern, thus inviting the male in.

In some species of orb-weaving spiders, the male will signal to the female via a special mating thread that he attaches to the periphery of her web. He continues

FACING PAGE
Male araneid spiders such as this marbled orb-weaver (Araneus marmoreus) *use chemical as well as tactile cues during courtship. While a male might finally attract a female to him by twanging and plucking her web, he might first have found her in part by following the chemical cues of her pheromone-scented silk.*
BILL BEATTY

A FEMALE GOLDEN ORB-WEB SPIDER (NEPHILA CLAVIPES) CAN WEIGH AS MUCH AS ONE HUNDRED MALES AND VIRTUALLY IGNORES MALES WHO COME TO CALL.

to signal her, trying to entice her out of her web and onto the mating thread. If she's interested, she'll eventually crawl out onto the thread and assume a position for mating. The male of one web-building species, *Metellina segmentata*, waits patiently, often for hours or even days, until an insect gets stuck in the female's web. Then, while she's preoccupied with her meal, he'll begin courtship and mating.

Some spiders dispense with all of the niceties of courtship once they've found a mate and instead get right to business. A male crab spider, for instance—which is minuscule compared with the female—essentially pounces on the female and, after some initial palpal strokes on her body, begins to mate. A female golden orb-web spider (*Nephila clavipes*) can weigh as much as one hundred males and virtually ignores males who come to call. It is thought that these males are so much smaller than the minimum size of her normal prey that she even ignores them as a potential meal. The males are so inconsequential that she allows them to crawl around on her, and in her web, and they need not fear being eaten.

The male European crab spider (*Xysticus cristatus*) also has few introductory gestures. His first act is to grab one of his mate's front legs, provoking a scuffle. Undeterred, he maintains his grip and then climbs onto her back and begins circling while stroking her with his legs. Although this is a fairly common gesture that seems to make females more receptive, this spider has an ulterior motive. As he circles, he trails a line of silk that ties her down and allows him to mate and then depart in safety. The female easily disentangles herself from this bondage after mating.

The submissiveness of females varies widely from one species to the next. Things are fairly straightforward with many funnel-web weavers (*Agelena* species). The long-legged male announces that he has arrived by tapping on her web. If she is ready to mate, she'll simply collapse and allow the male to drag her off to a place he finds suitable for mating.

FACING PAGE
The difference in size between the sexes in species of Nephila *is so great that males can safely venture into a female's web without danger of being eaten.*
GERTRUD & HELMUT DENZAU

The Reward

Finally, after the males have gone to quite a bit of trouble to get the females "in the mood," the spiders are ready for mating. Mating positions vary from one species to the next. As described above, tarantulas (and other mygalomorphs) usually approach each other from the front. The female rises, and the male inserts his palpal bulb in her genital pore, or epigynum. Although that sounds fairly straightforward, getting out of this position is a little more precarious. The female quickly turns from being receptive to being annoyed, and the wary male bolts out of her way as soon as he finishes mating.

In the six-eyed spiders and web-building spiders, the male approaches the female from the front; from there he dips his palpal bulb into her epigynum. This position works especially well with web-building spiders, since the female is usually hanging below the male in a position where she can do him little harm.

In wandering spiders, including wolf, crab, and jumping spiders, the male usually crawls on top of the female's body, reaches his palps around her, and inserts the palpal bulb into her epigynum. The male is also fairly safe in this position, and sometimes the female seems to ignore him completely; she may move around while he is firmly attached.

FACING PAGE

The inflated palpal bulbs of the male nursery-web spider (Pisaura mirabilis) *are clearly visible as he approaches a female for mating.*

HANS PFLETSCHINGER/ PETER ARNOLD INC.

Fatal Attraction

Males are generally adept at avoiding ornery females, but on occasion courtship can end with a male clenched in a final embrace in the female's jaws. This denouement is not as horrific as it might sound, however, since most males have short lives and may die soon after copulation anyway.

Female widow spiders are most commonly accused of having a taste for their spent mates. Although sexual cannibalism does occur, males often leave the web unharmed after mating. In fact, in some widow species, the males have been seen living, quite unharmed, in females' webs for weeks, even sharing a meal or two with their mate.

The Australian redback widow spider (*Latrodectus hasselti*) is one species where the propensity for the female to eat her mate is not overstated. Australian redback cannibalism, however, comes with a quirky twist—the male is devoured not after sex but *during* sex. While the male has his palpal bulb still inserted in the female, he turns a somersault and positions his abdomen in front of the female. The female often can't resist and starts chewing on her mate. Researchers think the female is now distracted from sex and is more interested in her meal. This distraction allows the male to copulate longer, giving his sperm a better chance to fertilize the next generation. So, although it may seem to be a curious strategy, since males usually mate only once, this technique gives them the best shot at reproductive success.

The male of the orb-weaver species *Araneus pallidus* also succumbs to his mate, but this result seems to be more a technical necessity than an altruistic strategy. After inserting his palpal bulb into the female's epigynum, the male, which is considerably smaller than the female, tumbles backwards and rests underneath her jaws. If she doesn't hang onto him, he continually slips off her abdomen, interrupting mating. To prevent this interruption, she slings a few strands of silk over him and ties him on, temptingly nestled in her jaws. After a few minutes of restraint, she delivers a poisoned "kiss" and begins to dine.

The jumping spider *Portia* adds another level of complexity to sexual suicide. After the male mounts the female, she spins a dragline and the pair mate suspended in midair. While dangling on this line, a female may lunge at the male with her fangs bared and then eventually kill and eat her mate.

The causes of sexual cannibalism are intriguing yet still relatively speculative. Although it is tempting to attribute sexual cannibalism to mistaken identity, this idea has been questioned for a couple of reasons. First, highly visual jumping spiders and orb-web spiders with elaborate communication strategies show high levels of sexual cannibalism. Second, although sexual cannibalism is fairly widespread among orb-web spiders, this behavior is virtually absent in other web-building spiders.

Researchers have developed a theoretical framework that explains the advantages and disadvantages in relation to the sex of the spider and the time that the cannibalism occurs. The model suggests that the encounter rate with the opposite sex and the nutritional value of the male in relation to other species of prey may determine the behavior. If there is a high density of males in an area, for instance, a female can a ord to dine on a few males before actually mating. She gains nutritional benefit without sacrificing her ultimate ability to reproduce. Another study showed that females cannibalized smaller males more often than larger males, each thereby increasing her fecundity while waiting for a male that she determined was suitably large for mating.

Even if they survive sex, male spiders are not likely to live much longer, since most spiders live only one year, or perhaps two. Mygalomorphs are the exception; female tarantulas can live for twenty years, and some purse-web spiders (*Atypus*) have survived for seven years. The newly mated females of all species, however, will live at least long enough to lay their eggs and to begin preparing for the arrival of the next generation.

AUSTRALIAN REDBACK CANNIBALISM, HOWEVER, COMES WITH A QUIRKY TWIST THE MALE IS DEVOURED NOT AFTER SEX BUT DURING SEX.

THE NEW GENERATION

After the female has received the male's sperm, she doesn't have to use it right away. In many species, sperm can be stored in the female's own personal sperm bank, a special reservoir in her abdomen. This strategy allows the female to fertilize and lay her eggs when she is ready. Some species stagger their egg laying, producing some eggs in the fall and more the following spring without having to mate in the interim. Others undergo repeated matings and lay multiple batches of eggs.

Because spiders are so closely identified with the use of silk, it is not surprising that the first action any female takes with her eggs is to swathe them in silk. In most spiders, the female first spins a flat silk saucer on which she will deposit her eggs. Next, she releases the stored sperm, which fertilizes the eggs internally before she squeezes them out the genital opening and onto their bed. To protect the eggs from parasites, desiccation, and predation, she further binds them in layers of silk to make a cocoon or egg sac.

The shape and size of egg sacs vary from one species to the next, as do the number and size of individual eggs laid. The tiny 2-millimeter-long (3⁄32-inch-long) *Oonops domesticus*, for instance, lays only two eggs, whereas some tarantulas lay over a thousand tapioca-sized eggs. One of the simplest egg sacs is that of the female long-bodied cellar spider, which holds her eggs together with a few strands of silk and carries them around in her jaws until they hatch. Nursery-web spiders

FACING PAGE
The production of the beautiful pear-shaped egg sac of the black-and-yellow garden spider (Argiope aurantia) *defies gravity. The female first spins a thick mat of silk on vegetation and then lays her eggs upwards into the nest. Next she will cover the eggs in several sheets of flocculent, curly silk and a final coating of parchment-like silk.*
ROBERT MCCAW

and spitting spiders also carry their egg sacs in their jaws, and a wolf spider mom attaches the egg sac to her spinnerets and carries it with her until the eggs hatch.

Female ground-dwelling tarantulas spend a considerable amount of time bundling their eggs. First the spider digs a bowl-shaped depression and lines it with a thick padding of silk. After depositing the eggs, she lays more silk over them and then gathers the edges of the original padding and begins rolling the egg sac. She continues to roll and "silk" the egg sac until she is satisfied with it.

Most female spiders fight valiantly if an attempt is made to remove their egg sac. The wolf spider seems to exhibit what humans might call a maternal instinct, for if she loses her egg sac she continues to have an overwhelming urge to carry something in her spinnerets. Anything approaching the right size and shape will do; female wolf spiders have "adopted" empty snail shells, cotton, and even rabbit droppings in lieu of an egg sac.

Still others guard the egg sacs, sometimes until death. A crab spider, for instance, creates her egg sac and then clasps it until she dies of starvation. The funnel-web weaver *Agelena labyrinthica* builds an elaborate silken labyrinth and then hides her egg sacs within the maze. She also guards her egg sacs until she dies. The green lynx spider (*Peucetia viridans*) takes a different approach and spits venom into the face of any predator approaching her progeny.

Other spiders abandon their egg sacs, usually only after they've taken special care to camouflage them. The sacs may be cryptically colored or covered in another type of material, such as bits of ground debris or mud plaster.

Growing Up

Inside each egg, developing young grow as they feed on the large yolk. When the egg becomes restrictive, they hatch with the aid of a tiny egg tooth and join their siblings wriggling inside the cocoon. The spiderlings continue to feed on their

FACING PAGE
The female green lynx spider (Peucetia viridans) *clings tightly to her enormous knobby egg sac as she hangs camouflaged in vegetation. Alternatively, she may attach the egg sac to a leaf and stand guard over it.*
BRIAN KENNEY

yolk reserves and eventually go through their first molt. Now, equipped with all they need to venture out into the world, the young cut their way out of the egg sac.

Some spiders continue to care for their young even after they've hatched from the egg sac. Wolf spider moms help their babies out of the egg sac by opening the rim of the cocoon. The young then climb onto her back, where up to a hundred spiderlings cling to her hairs. These special hairs are covered in curved spines and tipped with knobs—a sort of spider saddle horn. During this free ride the spiders continue to live off their yolk supply, until finally, after seven or eight days, they go through their second molt, signaling that it is time they set off on their own.

True to its name, the female nursery-web spider spins a silken tent for her spiderlings. When the young first emerge, they cluster near their mother, but they eventually disperse throughout their tent and finally leave the shelter altogether.

About twenty species of spider mothers feed their newly hatched young. The female of some species, such as the funnel-web spider *Coelotes*, simply drops prey for her young when they "beg" by touching her chelicerae with their palps or legs. If the prey is still moving, the mother won't release it from her jaws; she signals this message by vigorously beating her hind legs against the web. Other web-weaving spiders simply leave entangled prey in the web for their young, sometimes indicating its presence to them by plucking the web.

One of the most advanced forms of parental care in spiders is demonstrated by the European cob-web weaver (*Theridion sisyphium*), which feeds its young regurgitated food. Several other spiders, including some tarantulas and orb-weavers, exhibit this behavior as well. For the first few days of life out of the egg sac, the newly hatched spiderlings gather around the female's mouth and feed on the droplets of liquefied food. The young spiderlings can stimulate her to regurgitate by stroking her legs. After the spiderlings have gone through their first molt outside of

THE WOLF SPIDER SEEMS TO EXHIBIT WHAT HUMANS MIGHT CALL A MATERNAL INSTINCT. FOR IF SHE LOSES HER EGG SAC SHE CONTINUES TO HAVE AN OVERWHELMING URGE TO CARRY SOMETHING IN HER SPINNERETS.

FACING PAGE

Dozens of newly hatched wolf spiderlings (Lycosa *sp.) hitch a ride on their mother. If any babies happen to tumble off, they simply climb up their mother's legs to regain their mount. Within a week or so, they will set off on their own.*

STEPHEN KIRKPATRICK

FACING PAGE *After emerging from their egg sac, these tiny araenid spiderlings are equipped with all that they need to feed and to produce silk. To ensure adequate food and habitat for all, many will disperse by "ballooning," in which they hitch a ride on a strand of silk using the natural lift of rising warm air currents.* CSABA FORRÀSY

the egg sac, she stops feeding them directly and they begin to share prey. Eventually, she chases her offspring away to fend for themselves.

In an unusual act of biological efficiency, some spider mothers will die after the initial stages of care and allow their young to dine on their corpse. Why, after all, should a mother leave her corpse to a scavenger, when her own progeny could make use of it? But in one species, the Australian social spider *Diaea ergandros,* the young don't wait for Mom to die before starting their meal. In this unusual example of matriphagy, the mother at first cares for her young by bringing them large insects, up to ten times her own weight. Bringing this sizable meal not only provides her young with food but allows her to fatten up and store extra nutrients in unfertilized eggs. In an interview in *Discover* magazine, researcher Theodore Evans describes the mother as a living refrigerator. "When the weather cools and insects become more scarce, nutrients from the eggs seep into the mother's bloodstream. As the spiders get hungrier, they raid the fridge—sucking nutrient-rich blood from their unresisting mother's leg joints." Eventually they suck their mother dry, and she is weakened and unable to move. When she is this withered, they attack her as they would prey, injecting her with venom and then consuming her. Evans describes this spider's behavior as the ultimate form of parental care.

Moving On

> *I saw the spiders marching through the air,*
> *Swimming from tree to tree . . .*
>
> —ROBERT LOWELL, "Mr. Edwards and the Spider"

A few days after hatching, life can get a little crowded for spider siblings huddling near their egg sac. After their yolk reserves are depleted, the competition for

> TO AVOID HIGH LEVELS OF SIBLING CANNIBALISM, SPIDERS MUST DISPERSE.

available food heightens. To avoid high levels of sibling cannibalism, spiders must disperse. Dispersal can occur gradually, as the spiders migrate inch by inch away from their mother. Some even spin their own tiny webs and start to catch insects. But a more sudden and certainly spectacular type of dispersal takes place on sunny days when these flightless creatures take to the air. The phenomenon is known as ballooning. Although it was previously thought that only young spiders balloon, several adult spiders, including some with body lengths of up to 1 centimeter (3/8 inch), have been known to balloon.

Ballooning usually takes place on warm, rather than windy, days, when young spiders take advantage of thermal physics and take a ride on air rising from the warming earth. To begin their flight, the spiders usually climb onto a nearby promontory—a blade of grass or a fence post, for example. Next, they tilt their abdomen upwards and squeeze out a strand of silk, which is drawn upwards by the air currents, much as a kite string is. When the pull is strong enough for the young spiders to float in the air, they release their grip and take to the wind.

Although most spider flights are fairly short, perhaps a meter or two, some spiders take an incredible ride. These airborne travelers—called aeolian (aerial) plankton—ride at the mercy of the wind currents and as a consequence can find themselves far from home when the ride ends. Spiders have been captured in special traps affixed to aircraft as high as 4267 meters (14,000 feet), and Charles Darwin recorded the arrival of tiny red spiders when the *Beagle* was 97 kilometers (60 miles) off the coast of South America. Ballooning does more than ensure adequate food and habitat for young spiders, however; it also helps to recolonize devastated or newly created habitats.

After two-thirds of the island of Krakatau was destroyed in a volcanic eruption on August 27, 1883, most of the life on the island was either devastated in the explosion or covered in ash. Rakata, a mountain from the old island, survived, and nine months afterwards, a French expedition came searching for life. In his journals, the ship's naturalist wrote that "notwithstanding all my researches, I was not able to observe any symptoms of animal life. I only discovered one microscopic spider—only one; this strange pioneer of the renovations was busy spinning its web." Forty-eight years later, British arachnologist W. S. Bristowe revisited the island and counted over ninety species of spider. With the exception of three species, all of the species he found were known to disperse aerially. The other three species were found only in the huts imported by Dutch volcano experts.

A more recent study took place on Mt. St. Helens in Washington, where a volcanic eruption in 1980 effectively sterilized 80 square kilometers (30 square miles). A team of researchers monitored the arthropod fallout in the area and in one of the study sites found that 125 species had ballooned into the area. From knowledge of their present range and habitat, the team extrapolated that several species had traveled over 50 kilometers (30 miles) on the wind to recolonize the site.

Although spiders have no power over the direction of their flight, new research shows that they may have some control over its length. By rolling and shortening the thread or by drawing their legs close to their bodies, spiders can adjust their speed and rate of fall as they travel through the air. In addition, they are able to extend their flight and get greater "lift" by releasing new threads of silk.

Sheet-web weavers are skilled balloonists. On warm days it is not uncommon to see thousands of these spiders taking to the wind like an air force of miniature Mary Poppins. But the feather-light threads of silk—called gossamer—that float through the air and carpet large areas with silk have confused observers for centuries. Pliny the Elder remarked on a time when it "rained wool," and a shower of gossamer during World War II caused momentary panic when it was mistaken for chemical warfare.

TRULY SOCIAL SPIDERS

LIVE TOGETHER

IN COMPLEX WEBS

(USUALLY SHEET WEBS)

AND COOPERATE IN

CONSTRUCTING THE

WEBS AND CAPTURING

PREY.

SOCIAL SPIDERS

When spider webs unite, they can halt a lion.

—ETHIOPIAN PROVERB

Although spiders have the reputation of being solitary predators, who occasionally get together for somewhat perilous sex, about forty species of spiders live together in relatively peaceful colonies. These spiders are not simply a group of individuals that happen to be in the same area and that tolerate each other's existence; rather, they exhibit some level of cooperation. Web-weaving spiders are good candidates for social living, since they all live on their main source of communication—their webs.

Social behavior in spiders has two probable origins: prolonged mother-offspring associations, where offspring remain with the mother for an extended period, and aggregations of adult webs. The continuum of sociality ranges from mothers remaining with immature offspring to loose aggregations of webs to permanent web colonies with thousands of individuals.

Colonial spiders construct individual webs within a common framework. Cooperation in colonial species is usually limited to the construction of the web framework and some communal capturing of prey. Truly social spiders live together in complex webs (usually sheet webs) and cooperate in constructing the

FACING PAGE
The social spiders Cyrtophora *spin distinctive horizontally oriented webs en masse.*
GERTRUD & HELMUT DENZAU

FACING PAGE *Social spiders* Stegodyphus *share a meal. Their ability to hunt cooperatively allows these spiders to capture larger prey.* WOLFGANG BRAUNSTEIN

webs and capturing prey. They also engage in communal feeding and sometimes even share brood care.

Work by Dr. George Uetz has shown that the Mexican colonial spiders *Metepeira incrassata* construct individual webs within a common framework. These spiders can live in groups ranging from fifty to several thousand. The colonies span large areas, often on the periphery of coffee and banana plantations. Not surprisingly, communal living has costs as well as benefits. Foraging success is increased and spiders in the colony benefit from the ricochet effect, where prey that escapes capture in one web ricochets to another web, losing enough momentum to be caught. Because of the ricochet effect, colonial spiders can catch larger prey items. Colonial life also offers both adults and young spiders an increased level of protection from predators, by virtue of the sheer number of spiders. This advantage might quickly become a detriment if the prey supply is reduced, however. In these situations, a spider's predatory tendency could mean that a neighbor would become a meal instead of a dining partner.

Costs of colonial living include an increased vulnerability to predators and parasites due to the visibility and high density of the colony. One study demonstrated that the optimal size of a colony (measured by a high level of reproductive success) was one hundred to five hundred individuals. A smaller colony captured fewer prey, and, as a result, the females were not as fecund. Larger colonies showed levels of egg sac predation as high as 25 percent.

Where spiders construct their webs within the colony can also affect their survival. Spiders on the periphery of the colony, for instance, capture much more food but are also subject to higher levels of predation. Because predation is directed towards the larger spiders, larger individuals push for safer positions near the core of the colony. As a result, smaller individuals tend to reside on the periphery of the colony.

More complex social behavior is exhibited by several species of spiders that spin communal webs. Several hundred or even several thousand African funnel-web spiders (*Agelena consociata*) can share the same web. They distinguish one another from prey—which they will attack aggressively—by distinctive vibrations and pheromones. Another communal spider, *Anelosimus eximius,* a theridid common throughout Latin America, forms huge colonies of several thousand individuals sharing a web that can span several meters. These spiders move freely throughout the web, cooperatively capture large insects, and have a nursery area where many females guard the egg sacs.

Agelena consociata capture prey communally, but they do not always share it with the entire group. Prey may be grabbed by a solitary adult or by a group, depending on its size, but it is dragged off to a retreat by a single adult and is shared with as many spiders as can find space at the table. Other species are not so peaceful. The social *Stegodyphus* spiders, for instance, will hunt together, but when it comes to sharing the catch, the prey often becomes the prize in a miniature tug-of-war.

Interestingly, being in a group is not mandatory for all social species. In *Stegodyphus dumicola,* for instance, many individuals live solitary lives in small nests outside of the colony. One advantage of living in the colony, however, is that together spiders can overpower larger prey. Sociality tends to confer other benefits as well, including more-rapid growth, longer life expectancy, a lower death rate, and a smaller number of eggs. Fewer eggs may not at first seem to be an advantage, but this is a common trend in social animals. In social spiders, brood care is usually more successful; thus, fewer eggs are needed to perpetuate the species. As well, the more social the spider, the more skewed the sex ratios. In *Anelosimus eximius,* for example, there is only one male for every thirty to fifty females.

It was originally thought that all social spiders were web-weaving spiders because their webs were the perfect medium for communication. Recently, however, social crab, lynx, and huntsman spiders have been recorded. The fact that sociality has evolved independently in such a variety of spider families is an intriguing fact for scientists to ponder. The lynx spider *Tapinillus*, for instance, lives in a communal nest with several dozen relatives and cooperates in prey capture, brood care, and web maintenance. Although the social aspect of their lives is of interest, so is the fact that these spiders—normally solitary hunters—are spinning webs at all. Perhaps this fact points to some evolutionary link between web building and social behavior.

Part Three
WELCOME TO MY PARLOR: SPIDER PREDATION

the silk hardens, and it crosses,
tiptoe, the tiny span,
eager to turn mummies
from wing crisp to liquid caramel

—DIANE ACKERMAN, "Spiders"

Spiders are always on a liquid diet. Rather than chewing and swallowing their food and letting digestive juices dissolve it internally, the spider delivers digestive juices to its dinner before ingesting it. This technique predigests the prey, allowing the spider to suck in a liquid meal.

The spider's first task is to subdue its struggling prey, which it does by delivering a venomous bite. The venom can either kill or paralyze the prey. Once the prey is quelled—thus minimizing the damage it can do to the spider or to its home—the spider can get down to the business of eating.

How a spider devours its prey depends on the species and on the apparatus available to it. Comb-footed spiders and crab spiders puncture an insect's exoskeleton with their fangs and pump digestive enzymes into the insect, liquifying its tissues. The spider then uses its special sucking stomach, which works something like a water pump, to consume its meal. Hairs on the chelicerae and in the pharynx filter the food, and the captured particles are washed back out with the digestive

FACING PAGE
This bee didn't stand a chance against the female golden orb-weaver (Nephila clavipes), *one of the largest araneomorph spiders.*
JEFF FOOTT/ BBC NATURAL HISTORY UNIT

FACING PAGE
The remains of a wolf spider's dinner reveal the entrance to its hideaway.
RICO & RUIZ / BBC NATURAL HISTORY UNIT

fluid. With this style of feeding there is very little external damage to the insect, and other than the fact that the insect is dead and has two tiny punctures in its body, it looks the same as it did before it blundered into the spider's path.

The same can't be said about prey that encounters most other spiders, which use teeth on the base of their chelicerae to mash and grind their prey. After the insect is crushed, a spider regurgitates digestive juices onto the victim and subsequently sucks in the soupy meal. Some spiders, including tarantulas, partially wrap their meal in a package of silk so that it remains together as the tissues dissolve and the limbs fall apart.

Spiders have inhabited earth for close to 400 million years, and during this time they've devised a formidable arsenal of techniques for capturing prey. Some lie in wait and then ambush their prey. Others snare their meal in webs of silk, and still others actively stalk and pounce on prey. Spitting, fishing, lassooing, and stealing are some of the more outrageous methods used by spiders to capture food.

LURKERS

Many spiders are sit-and-wait predators—they lurk, well hidden, waiting for prey to pass by. Trapdoor spiders (Ctenizidae), for instance, wait motionless just below their silken trapdoor, with four legs forward and four legs safe inside the retreat. When prey trundles by, the spider springs out and grabs it and then drags it into the burrow below. These spiders can react at lightning speed: some can lunge and capture their prey in only 0.03 seconds.

Spiders that use this ambush style of prey capture sense approaching prey in several ways. Some intercept vibrations on the ground using sensory hairs and extremely fine hairs called trichobothria. Others set up booby traps by creating silken trip wires that radiate out from the burrow entrance. Prey may stumble over the threads, or the spider may detect the prey's vibrations through the silk motion detectors.

Most tarantulas hunt by staying close to their burrows and taking advantage of prey that happens by. Although the bulk of their diet consists of insects and other arthropods (including spiders), larger species have been known to kill and eat larger prey, including mice, frogs, and snakes. Occasionally arboreal tarantulas capture birds and bats, although this behavior is thought to be uncommon. Swiss naturalist Maria Sibylla Merian recorded the first account of bird-eating spiders in 1705; in her book on the insects of Suriname, she illustrated a pinktoe tarantula (*Avicularia* sp.) eating a hummingbird. Merian's report was received with great

FACING PAGE
When the lid capping this trapdoor spider's burrow is closed, its home is virtually invisible. As night falls, these nocturnal hunters gently raise the top of their silken retreats and await passing prey.
HANS CHRISTOPH KAPPEL / BBC NATURAL HISTORY UNIT

CRAB SPIDERS HAVE ONE OF THE MOST TOXIC SPIDER VENOMS, AND ARE ONE OF THE FEW SPIDERS THAT INCLUDE VENOMOUS WASPS AND BEES ON THEIR MENU.

skepticism, as it was not believed that spiders could eat vertebrates. Corroboration of Merian's report came years later when another naturalist, H. W. Bates, observed and recorded a spider's capture and killing of a sparrow. Even though these naturalists had both witnessed a behavior that is probably quite rare, British naturalists adopted the name "bird-eating spiders" for tarantulas; the name is still sometimes used today.

Purse-web spiders spend most of their lives sealed in their silken tubes, which rest partially exposed above ground. Except when males wander in search of receptive females, purse-web spiders rarely leave this home, even to catch dinner. Instead, they wait for an insect to walk across the top of the tube and then stab it through the silk with their sharp chelicerae. While they inject paralyzing venom, they simultaneously use their chelicerae to saw a hole through the silken tube, before dragging their prey inside. After storing the meal, the spiders mend the hole with their silk.

Crab spiders are known for their tendency to lie in wait, camouflaged and motionless, on flowers, although they are also found on bark or on the ground. When an insect alights nearby, the crab spider furtively moves into the best position to strike at the victim's head. Crab spiders have one of the most toxic spider venoms, and are one of the few spiders that include venomous wasps and bees on their menu. Occasionally a crab spider will take a flight on its victim's back if the poison is slow to work. This trip is short-lived, however, as both victim and spider fall to the ground when the toxins kick in.

FACING PAGE
Although insects are most often on the menu of spiders, some species are able to capture vertebrate prey. This gecko fell prey to a wheel spider (Carparachne aureoflava).
MICHAEL & PATRICIA FOGDEN

REMARKABLY, JUMPING SPIDERS HAVE EVEN BEEN SEEN LEAPING OFF VERTICAL SURFACES, WHILE ANCHORED BY A BUNGEE CORD OF SILK, TO CAPTURE INSECTS IN FLIGHT.

HUNTERS

Wolf spiders, jumping spiders, and lynx spiders are all excellent hunters. They are active during the day and rely on their large and efficient front eyes to find prey. After they locate a potential meal, they slowly creep forward, catlike, until they're within pouncing distance. Jumping spiders have the most acute sight of any spiders and can pounce on prey from a distance of twenty times their body length. Remarkably, jumping spiders have even been seen leaping off vertical surfaces, while anchored by a bungee cord of silk, to capture insects in flight. The strand of silk not only provides the spider with a route back to its starting point but also offers a base to leverage off while they assault the prey.

FACING PAGE
Before takeoff, jumping spiders, including this species of Phidippus, *attach a silk safety line to the ground or vegetation to ensure a route back to the starting point.*
DWIGHT KUHN

TRAPPERS

The spinning of an orb-web is a spectacle to be watched and watched and watched.

—T. H. SAVORY, *The Spider's Web*

FACING PAGE

How can funnel-web spiders move so quickly across their webs while insects walk so clumsily? A closer look at agelenid spiders reveals that they run on "tiptoe," thus limiting contact with the web. Insects have a more "flat-footed" walk, which increases adhesion and hampers movement.

DWIGHT KUHN

Over three thousand known species of spiders (in the families Araneidae, Tetragnathidae, Theridiosomatidae, and Uloboridae) spin orb webs, and each has its own subtle differences on the overall design, which provide clues useful for spider identification. Within each web style there are also variations in the number of radii, closeness of spirals, and ornamentation. These intricate web designs are under tight genetic control, and, remarkably, a baby orb-weaver can spin a perfect orb web soon after it leaves the egg sac. Other than making periodic, minor modifications to suit the size or attachment site of the web, the spider will not change the web throughout its life.

Sheet webs are used by a variety of spiders, including sheet-web weavers (Linyphiidae) and funnel-web weavers (Agelenidae), and are particularly common in temperate zones. Sagging hammock webs or taut sheet webs are a common sight on lawns and meadows. Some species also pull their sheet web up into a dome. Often the spiders construct a tangled maze of threads above the web—called scaffolding or knock-down threads—which unsuspecting insects blunder into. Linyphiid spiders wait underneath the silken sheet and spear their victims

BOLAS SPIDERS (MASTOPHORA) ARE ORB-WEAVING SPIDERS (FAMILY ARANEIDAE) THAT HAVE DISPENSED WITH ALL BUT A SINGLE LINE FOR THEIR WEBS.

through the web and then pull them down through the sheet. Funnel-web spiders use a similar web and trapping technique, although they wait for their prey at the entrance to a silken tunnel that leads off to one side of the web. These spiders construct a sturdier web than do the linyphiids and can run across the top of the sheet to capture prey. Some mygalomorph spiders also spin sheet webs.

The rather untidy scaffold webs, or cobwebs, of theridiid spiders (including widow spiders) are composed of a mass of intersecting threads. Although at first glance a web of this type looks as if it has been constructed haphazardly, there is a pattern to its design. Supporting threads act as guy-wires and attach the web to the substrate above it, such as a ceiling or a piece of wood. Trap threads attach to the ground below the web and are studded with droplets of glue. When an insect touches a trap thread, the thread breaks, suspending the helpless insect in the air.

Some "webs" are as simple as a single thread or two. The location of sticky glue globules varies, or there may not be any glue at all, but remarkably, these "reduced" webs are highly effective and catch more insects per thread than more complex webs. Bolas spiders (*Mastophora*) are orb-weaving spiders (family Araneidae) that have dispensed with all but a single line for their webs. With astounding accuracy and skill, bolas spiders use this line as a lasso and swing it at passing insects. A sticky ball at the end of the line is coated in a pheromone mimicking that of a female moth, and not surprisingly, much of the diet of these spiders is composed of male moths.

The web construction of the common garden spider, *Araneus diadematus*, has been closely observed and well described. The spider's first task is to spin the strong bridging line that will suspend the entire web. There are two techniques for creating this line. The first is to walk the line across the space in which the web will be built, by climbing across vegetation to get to the attachment site, all the while trailing a dragline. The second method is to use air currents, emitting a silk thread until it catches on the far side of the space. Once the line has caught, the spider pulls it taut, anchors it, and then walks back and forth across the bridge, spinning new strands of silk to make a strong cable.

On its final pass along the bridge line, the spider trails looser line that it will fix at either end of the bridge. The spider then crawls along the drooping line and, at its midpoint, attaches a new strand of silk and drops down to form a Y-shaped frame, called the first fork.

The spider now uses this frame as a base and begins the task of laying up to fifty radiating spokes from the web's hub. (Whereas araneids use up to fifty radii, other spiders can use more. *Cyrtophora* sp., for instance, have up to two hundred radii in their webs.) Next the spider crawls to the center of the web and begins to spin a temporary, widely spaced "scaffolding" spiral, using its legs to measure the spaces between each turn. Until this point, all of the threads have been made of dry silk. Now, however, the spider retraces its steps, bundling and eating the threads of the scaffolding spiral while it replaces them with sticky threads. As each of the sticky threads is attached to one of the radii, or spokes, the spider snaps the line to spread the sticky coating into a series of evenly spaced droplets, like a row of pearls.

The design of both the web and the web-weaving spider answer the oft-asked question "Why don't spiders get stuck in their own webs?" They *can* get stuck in their own webs, but only if they are not in control of their movements and fall into contact with the sticky threads. (You'd almost have to throw them into the threads.) For the most part, orb-weavers travel along the dry threads of their web with the aid of two claws and the hook that tips each leg. When they travel on sticky threads, however (which they must do to gather prey), the spiders tiptoe around the glue. Getting a bit of the adhesive on their feet is not much more of a problem for them than stepping into a wad of gum is for a human. But if the spider—or the prey the web was intended for—slams into the web uncontrollably, it comes into contact with about fifty droplets of glue, enough to make it stick.

Some orb-weavers adorn the center of their webs with decorative bands or zigzags of fuzzy hackle-band silk in a structure called the stabilimentum. As the name suggests, this structure was originally thought to strengthen and stabilize the web. This theory is now disputed. Although there is no consensus as to the structure's definitive purpose, the stabilimentum probably has several functions. Some studies have shown that birds avoid flying through webs adorned with a stabilimentum, so the structure may be an early-warning signal to prevent web destruction. Another theory suggests that the stabilimentum reflects ultraviolet light just as flowers do, and so it may attract insects. Others propose that the structure may provide camouflage or may make the spider appear larger. In desert species the stabilimentum is thought to act as a parasol to shelter spiders from the sun.

SPECIALISTS

Many types of spiders specialize in eating other spiders. Araneophagy is routine for a few spider families, the pirate spiders (Mimetidae) being one of the better known. Pirate spiders can mimic the movements a struggling insect might make in the web and lure the unsuspecting resident spider perilously close. Some can even mimic the courtship twangs of a male spider from a different species, hoping to trick the resident female. Pirate spiders also steal insects from other spiders' webs and will open and eat the contents of egg sacs.

The jumping spider *Portia* is unusual in that it builds a web and hunts freely. This spider can also mimic the signals of trapped prey and the mating tunes of some spiders. Researchers Robert Jackson and Stim Wilcox wondered how *Portia* could match these signals—which are fine-tuned and specific to each spider—so beautifully. They discovered that *Portia* "learned" by trial and error—a skill that no other spider is known to have and that only a few other invertebrates share.

Portia has also perfected its ability to stalk and attack prey. When stalking prey it sways gently, resembling a leaf blowing in the wind. Its stalking technique, as well as its camouflage coloring, is so convincing that even other jumping spiders—noted for their acute vision—don't notice *Portia*. When it is close to its prey, the spider lunges and bites with an especially potent poison. Within thirty seconds, a spider is paralyzed, whereas, curiously, the venom takes up to four minutes to affect insect prey. *Portia*'s success as a predator, even of spiders, lies in its combination of skills—excellent vision, cryptic coloring, slow, robotlike motion, a deadly lunge, and powerful venom.

THE HUNTER AS HUNTED

Wasps are one of spiders' main predators. Spider wasps (pompilids, sphecids), as their name suggests, are spider-hunting specialists, and their tactics are fodder for any horror film. Although most species of spider wasp feed on nectar as adults, they all get their start in life by feeding on a spider's live body. A female spider wasp first paralyzes a spider with her sting. Next, the wasp drags the spider back to her retreat, where she lays an egg on the spider's abdomen. The egg eventually hatches into a larva that feeds on the still-living spider. Eventually the spider succumbs to this assault, but it may survive for weeks or even months as a living larder for the wasp larvae. Other wasps, including mud daubers and ichneumonid wasps, also attack adult spiders and sometimes lay their eggs in spider cocoons. The formidable *Pepsis* wasps, with a body length of 8 centimeters (3 inches), are species-specific predators of tarantulas. Seeing one of these wasps attacking a tarantula might elicit some sympathy in even the most die-hard arachnophobe.

Several types of vertebrates also prey on spiders. Fish, toads, reptiles, and birds feed on spiders, as do several mammals, including monkeys, coatimundis, shrews, and bats. In addition, many small birds, especially hummingbirds, steal the webs of spiders and use them to bind their nests. Cribellate, or hackle-band, silk is most commonly used, since its fuzzy texture makes it useful for attaching material such as lichens or leaves to the nest.

To try to minimize attacks from natural enemies, spiders have evolved a

FACING PAGE

To escape predators, the wheel spider (Carparachne aureoflava) *rolls down sand dunes by flipping its body sideways and cartwheeling over its bent legs. For this spider, the escape technique failed and a predatory pompilid wasp prepares to lay her eggs on the spider's paralyzed but still-living body.*

MICHAEL & PATRICIA FOGDEN

ALTHOUGH MOST SPECIES OF SPIDER WASP FEED ON NECTAR AS ADULTS, THEY ALL GET THEIR START IN LIFE BY FEEDING ON A SPIDER'S LIVE BODY.

number of survival strategies, the most obvious of which is to avoid being noticed in the first place. Subterranean dwellers such as the mygalomorphs are the specialists in this strategy, and their burrows range from a simple hole in the ground to an elaborate fortress with complicated arrangements of doors and branched burrows. Some have gone one step further to avoid attack. The Australian trapdoor spider (*Anidiops villosus*), for instance, piles its garbage—mostly discarded prey—in a collapsible sock in the neck of its burrow. If threatened, the spider runs below the sock and pulls the debris down, effectively sealing the burrow from further penetration. The wolf spider *Arctosa* seals the entrance to its burrow with a silken curtain that hangs, ready to be drawn in a flash, at the burrow entrance. Should a predator still be able to enter the burrow, as wasps often can, *Arctosa* may be able to escape through a hidden passage, the other branch in its Y-shaped burrow.

Other spiders use cryptic coloring to make them invisible to predators. With the exception of a few species, most spiders, especially females, are demurely dressed in browns, grays, and blacks. Their subdued or mottled patterns make them quite invisible on vegetation and bark or among stones. Two-tailed spiders (Hersiliidae), giant crab spiders (Heteropodidae), and other spiders that live on tree bark have gone one step further and have a flattened body as well as camouflage coloring. Their flattened bodies reduce the amount of shadow they cast.

Still other spiders reduce their visibility by mimicking items that would be less attractive to a potential predator. Certain crab spiders mimic bird droppings, and other spiders mimic twigs or leaves, for example. Several tropical spiders have hit upon the perfect solution—they mimic, almost identically, ants that are routinely rejected by most predators. Some ant mimics go so far as to live within the ants' nest or at least in the same vicinity.

If spiders are caught in the open, some can exhibit aggressive displays in a last-ditch attempt to ward off the predators. The larger mygalomorph trapdoor

FACING PAGE
This spider's stunning combination of cryptic colors and distinctive patterning (which breaks up the body shape into smaller units) camouflages it against its tree bark habitat. This spider was photographed on the Omo River in Ethiopia.
GAVRIEL JECAN / ART WOLFE INC.

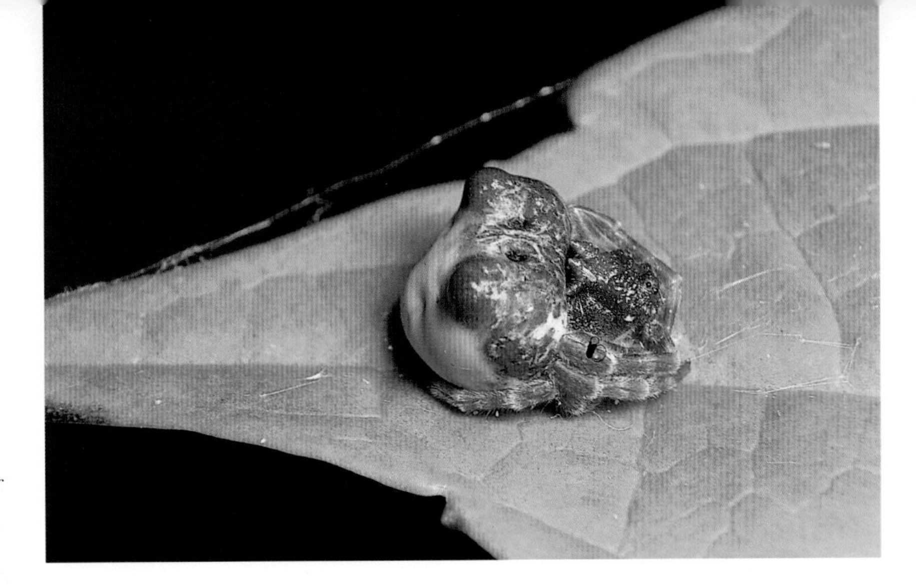

FACING PAGE

Several hundred species of spiders copy the shape, the coloration, and sometimes even the movements of ants. Only on closer inspection do the two body parts and eight legs reveal the creature's true identity as a spider.

PREMAPHOTOS/ BBC NATURAL HISTORY UNIT

ABOVE

With her legs tucked close to her body, this female bolas spider (Mastophora sp.) *could easily be mistaken for a bird dropping as she waits motionless on a leaf for passing prey.*

JAMES H. ROBINSON

spiders and tarantulas strike a formidable pose of aggression, rearing up on their hind legs and exposing their fangs. And many spiders, if threatened, will simply bite and use their venom on the intruder. Others take advantage of their body fluids. The green lynx spider (*Peucetia viridans*) spits venom at enemies, and some of the larger South American mygalomorph spiders are purported to be able to squirt a chalky liquid from their anuses.

"New World" tarantulas have a further arsenal—their upper abdomen is covered with dartlike hairs called urticating hairs. These tiny hairs are scraped off the body with the hind legs by an irritated tarantula. Released into the air in a pufflike cloud, the urticating hairs are especially effective on the mucous membranes of the eyes and noses of mammals. These tiny quills cause extreme inflammation, as unprepared tarantula owners can attest.

Many spiders have developed specific defensive strategies for their unique set of circumstances. One spider, for example, has even discovered the wheel. The wheel spider (*Carparachne aureoflava*) lives in the African desert, and its archenemies are spider wasps. Wheel spiders can't run away from the wasps fast enough, but they've discovered that by rolling down the steep slopes of the desert, they *can* roll out of reach. These tiny 1.25-centimeter (½-inch) spiders can hit speeds of 0.5 to 1.5 meters (1½ to 5 feet) per second, meaning that they average twenty revolutions per second, roughly equivalent to the revolutions of the wheel of a car traveling at 220 kilometers (137 miles) per hour.

Finally, it is appropriate that even as a defensive strategy spiders turn to their

skill as inveterate spinners. Some web-weaving spiders will violently shake their webs when they are disturbed. Daddy-longlegs spiders can tremble so vigorously in their webs that they become virtually invisible. Silk lifelines, the draglines, are paid out behind most spiders wherever they travel. If spiders are threatened, they suddenly drop to the ground on the silk line. Many spiders will then pull their legs close to their bodies and "play dead" in a behavior called catalepsy. When all is clear, the spiders will ascend their silk climbing rope.

FACING PAGE
A female tarantula (Poecilotheria regalis) *strikes a formidable defense pose.* RICK WEST

Part Four
REVERED AND REVILED: PEOPLE AND SPIDERS

[Spiders are] the Jekylls and Hydes of the animal world, so deeply and in such different ways have their individualities impressed themselves on man.

—W. S. BRISTOWE, *The World of Spiders*

Spiders suffer from poor public relations, and people tend to have a rather fickle attitude towards them. Discovering a spider under clothes tossed on the floor or meeting one in the bathtub can evoke what psychologists call a disgust response in many of us, yet who can resist admiring a dew-laden orb-web on a cool morning? Our ambivalence is perhaps typified by the symbolism of the web—an artistic wonder that can lead to entrapment and death.

FACING PAGE
A banded argiope (Argiope trifasciata) *adorns the top of a gayfeather plant wth a garland of silk.* ROBERT MCCAW

SPIDERS IN FOLKLORE

Someone saw a spider hanging from a thread and that was the start of a story.

—SHIRLEY CLIMO, *Someone Saw a Spider*

FACING PAGE
Spiders' skill as spinners and weavers and their dogged persistence at their tasks (waiting patiently and motionless for prey) has made them the focus of folklore, legends, and myths around the world. This spider (Paraplectana sp.) *from the Amazon rain forest is a stunning example of how diverse and surprisingly beautiful spiders can be.*
MICHAEL & PATRICIA FOGDEN

Folklore from around the world explains, and often exaggerates, the duality of spiders in the human mind. For centuries in Europe and Britain, for instance, spiders were blamed for everything from food and water poisoning to plagues. Many spider bites were considered lethal, yet spider silk, and even spiders themselves, were often used in medical treatments. Longfellow's epic poem *Evangeline* makes reference to curing a fever "by wearing a spider hung round one's neck in a nutshell. . . ." Little Miss Muffet's aversion to spiders apparently arose from the enthusiasm with which her physician-father dispensed spider-based remedies.

Spiders have been seen as forecasters of weather (if you step on a spider, you'll bring on rain) and omens of good luck ("Spider in the corner, money in the chest"). Many cultures also tell stories of spiders that provided the inspiration for continued perseverance at a task. Scotland's Robert the Bruce, for instance, was apparently motivated to rally his men and defeat the English after he watched a spider doggedly try to construct a web across the entrance to a cave where he was hiding. Spiders were even seen as saviors, and stories from various countries tell of people, including the infant Christ, who were saved because a spider spun a web

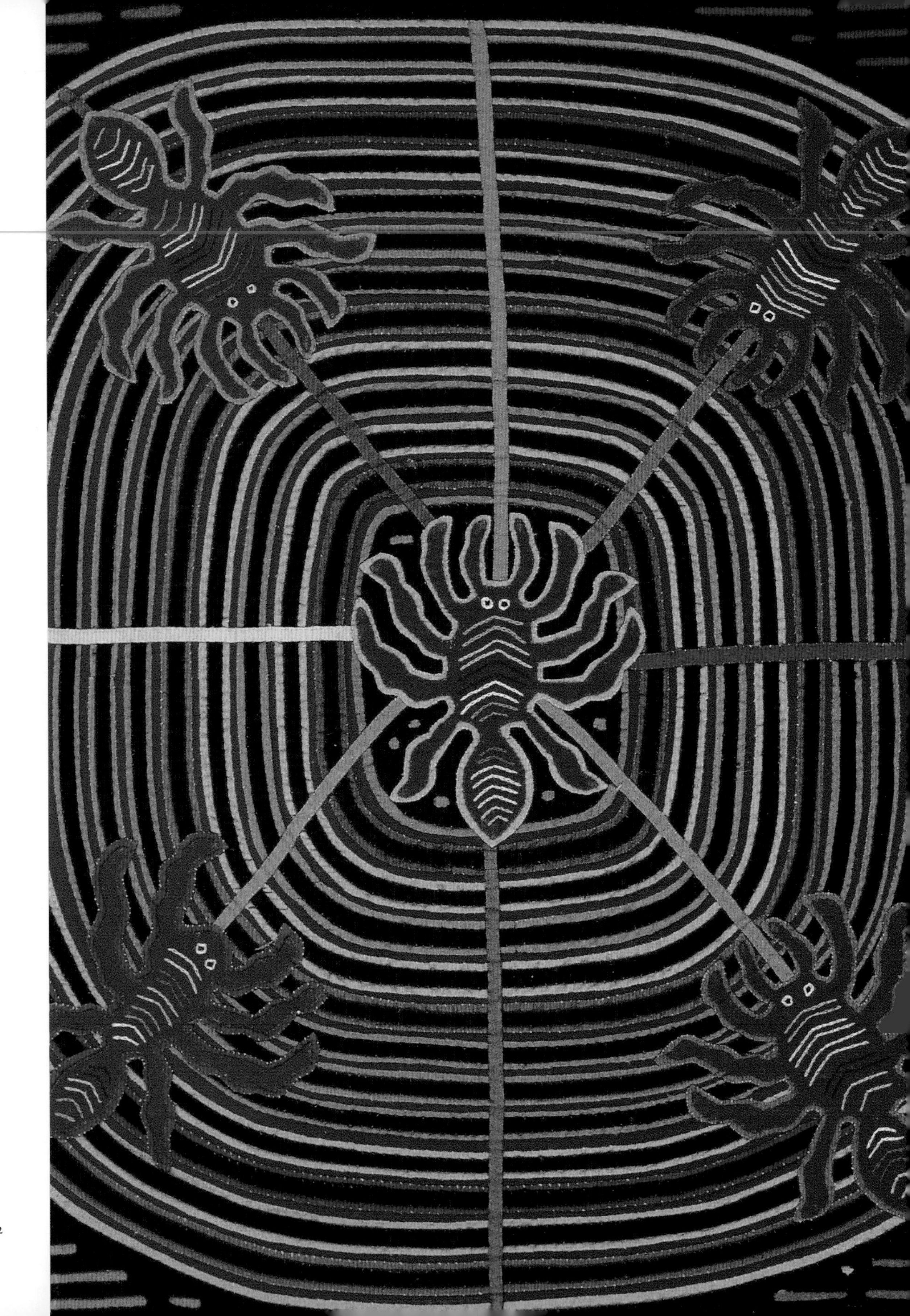

across the entrance to their hideout, usually a cave or hollow tree. The pursuers determined that because the web was intact, no one was behind it.

African, Asian, Caribbean, and Native American cultures are rich in stories of Grandmother Spider, Spider Woman, Ti-Jean, and Anansi; these stories represent the spider as trickster, creator, and wise weaver. Spiders are often central characters in creation stories and also play a part in the journey of souls after death. Many Native American stories tell of spiders spinning webs that connect the earth to the sky, providing souls with a silken ladder to the spirit world above.

According to the Navajo, it was Spider Woman who gave them their exceptional gift as weavers by way of a Pueblo girl who lived among them. The girl wandered away from her village and discovered a hole in the ground with smoke coming from it. This was the home of Spider Woman. Spider Woman invited the girl in and taught her how to weave. The girl, in turn, delivered her new-found knowledge to the Navajo community. The Navajo remember Spider Woman by leaving a small hole in their baskets, blankets and other woven items. The hole represents the entrance to Spider Woman's burrow in recognition of her gift.

FACING PAGE *Spider images are used in historic and contemporary art, including jewelry, pottery, and fabrics. This fabric* mola *is from San Blas, Panama.* FROM THE COLLECTION OF MICHAEL H. ROBINSON. PHOTOGRAPH BY JESSIE COHEN/NATIONAL ZOO

CONSERVING SPIDERS

If you wish to live and thrive
Let the spider run alive

—TRADITIONAL ENGLISH RHYME

Through the ages, spider folklore delivered healthy doses of both reverence and fear about spiders, but it also seemed to offer common sense. Traditional rhymes such as the one above and other folklore warning people against killing spiders indicate that there was some recognition of spiders' formidable ability as insect predators.

"We would be up to our butts in flies," tarantula expert Rick West jokes when he's asked to imagine a world without spiders. It is largely due to spiders' predatory tendency that insect populations are estimated to suffer mortality rates nearing 99 percent. Hypothetical calculations suggest that the spiders living on 1 hectare (2½ acres) of land devour over 47,500 kilograms (104,500 pounds) of prey each year, most of which is insects and other spiders. W. S. Bristowe estimated that the weight of insects consumed by spiders annually in Britain exceeded that of its human inhabitants.

The efficacy of spiders as predators naturally leads to thoughts of using them to control insect pests. Since most spiders are generalist predators, however, their

FACING PAGE
A red-eyed vireo delivers a snack of spider to its young. Spiders are a major source of prey for birds, particularly during winter and spring.
ROBERT MCCAW

ability to target a specific species is limited. In addition, spiders do not discriminate between insects that humans deem beneficial or detrimental. Although spiders' role in biological control has not been explicitly demonstrated in natural settings, in agriculture they have been shown to successfully control the high numbers of insect pests found in these managed areas. Since spiders are at present so poorly studied in most parts of the world, it is difficult to get a clear picture of their overall impact. No doubt it is significant, based on their sheer numbers, diversity of habits, and ability to successfully inhabit almost every ecological niche. Other ecological roles of spiders include their use as a food source by a variety of animals, including birds, mammals, and fish, and the use of spider silk in the nests of several families of birds.

Today we also seek to understand spiders' skill with silk and venom. Researchers interested in natural materials study the complex properties of spider silks in the hope that one day they will be able to duplicate their incredible combination of strength and flexibility. Spider venoms are being examined for possible inclusion in our own pharmacopoeia of medicines. More than twenty spider venoms are being studied for their potential applications as anti-epileptics, pain suppressors, and medications for patients suffering from Alzheimer's disease or stroke.

It is largely due to spiders' predatory tendency that insect populations are estimated to suffer mortality rates nearing 99 percent.

THREATS TO SPIDERS

The primary threat to spiders is the loss and degradation of habitat. Deforestation, agriculture, grazing, and urbanization have been shown to reduce the abundance of spiders, change the composition of spider communities, and affect spiders' food supplies. The use of pesticides, which kill beneficial insects and spiders as well as the targeted insect pests, also poses a real danger to the health of spider populations.

In fact, we know relatively little about the spiders now inhabiting the earth. Several species have been thoroughly studied, but some estimates suggest that well over 100,000 species of spiders are yet to be found. How many species are vanishing before they've even been discovered? Recent work in the canopies of old-growth temperate forests in the Pacific Northwest demonstrates this dilemma. When researchers examined the invertebrate communities living in mats of moss in the forest canopy, they captured thousands of arthropods, including insects, spiders, and mites. In just three valleys researcher Neville Winchester and his colleagues found over seventy species of spiders. Depending on the site, twenty-eight to thirty-two spiders were specific to the canopy habitat, a handful of which were previously undescribed species. Although the three valleys sampled were of similar habitat types, the composition of spider species varied significantly from one valley to the next. Only five species of spiders, for example, were found in all three valleys; all of the other species differed from site to site. Researchers speculate that there may be up to five hundred new and undescribed species of spiders and arthropods in these study sites alone.

Because relatively few scientists study spiders and the public generally lacks an understanding of spiders, only a small number of species have been deemed worthy of concern. For spiders to be seen as endangered, people must know about their current populations and distribution—rarely the case with spiders. The world populations and ecology of spiders are poorly understood, not so much for want of scientific interest, but more for the lack of opportunities for scientists to obtain employment studying spiders.

A handful of spiders, however, have found their way onto lists of threatened species, such as the Red List, compiled by the International Union for the Conservation of Nature and Natural Resources (IUCN). The 1996 IUCN Red List of Threatened Animals identifies nine spider species as vulnerable or at risk. In the United States, two species of spider are listed under the U.S. Endangered Species Act. The Tooth Cave spider of Texas (*Neoleptoneta myopica*), for example, is threatened because of destruction of its cave habitat (by causes that include flooding from sewer overflow) and predation by non-native fire ants. The spruce-fir moss spider (*Microhexura montivaga*) is also endangered because of loss of habitat, in part due to forest destruction by acid rain.

As a result of the pet trade in tarantulas, several species have been identified as potentially threatened and are listed in Appendix II of the Convention on International Trade in Endangered Species (CITES), which strictly regulates the import and export of these species. The first spider to be listed was the Mexican redknee tarantula (*Brachypelma smithi*), a colorful, docile spider that makes the ideal exotic pet. The female spiders were being dug out of their burrows and sold or smuggled out of the country. Not only was there concern that populations were being decimated (in part because of the huge numbers being harvested but also because only

FACING PAGE
The Mexican redknee tarantula is one of only a handful of spiders listed as threatened or endangered. Given the increased pace of habitat destruction and our relatively poor understanding of spider species and populations, one wonders how many other spiders deserve protective measures. Or, perhaps more disturbing, how many species have been lost before even being discovered?
BILL IVY / IVY IMAGES

females were being taken), but habitat was being destroyed by the wanton nature of the digging. After the Mexican redknee was successfully listed in CITES, work began to get other species included. To date, fifteen species, all tarantulas, are strictly regulated by the CITES list.

To prevent the illegal trafficking that often results when an animal becomes difficult to obtain, several proactive projects are under way to enable collectors to obtain tarantulas without decimating the species or ruining habitat. In Colima, Mexico, for instance, controlled breeding farms are being opened so that local residents can legally gather and raise tarantulas for the pet trade while boosting the local economy.

With so many species dwelling in such a diversity of habitats, the ultimate survival of spiders as a group is not in question. (The extinction of local populations is very real, however.) Long after we have cut our last tree, drained our last wetland, or perhaps even populated ourselves out of a home, somewhere, I have no doubt, spiders will be spinning. Their diversity, industry, and skill seems without parallel; after 400 million years, they have secured their place as one of nature's most successful terrestrial animals.

FOR FURTHER READING

Benyus, Janine. *Biomimicry*. New York: William Morrow, 1977.

Bristowe, W. S. *The World of Spiders*. London: Collins, 1976.

Comstock, J. H. *The Spider Book*. Ithaca, London: Comstock Publishing Associates, 1980.

Conniff, R. *Spineless Wonders: Strange Tales from the Invertebrate World*. New York: Henry Holt and Company, 1996.

Evans, Theodore. [Interview.] *Discover Magazine*, November 1995, 32–34.

Fabre, J.-Henri. *The Life of the Spider*. New York: Dodd, Mead and Co., 1914.

Foelix, R. F. *Biology of Spiders*. New York and Oxford: Oxford University Press, 1996.

Gertsch, W. J. *American Spiders*. New York: Van Nostrand Reinhold, 1979.

Hillyard, P. *The Book of the Spider: A Compendium of Arachno-facts and Eight-Legged Lore*. New York: Avon Books, 1998.

Jackson, Robert R. "Eight-Legged Tricksters." *Bioscience* 42, no. 8 (1992): 590–98.

Jackson, Robert R. "*Portia* Spider: Mistress of Deception." *National Geographic*, November 1996, 104–15.

Levi, H. W., and H. S. Levi. *Spiders and Their Kin*. New York: Golden Press, 1987.

Marshall, S. D. *Tarantulas and Other Arachnids*. Hauppauge, N.Y.: Barron's, 1996.

Preston-Mafham, R., and K. Preston-Mafham. *Spiders of the World*. New York: Blandford Press, 1984.

APPENDIX: A GUIDE TO COMMON SPIDER FAMILIES

SUBORDER MYGALOMORPHAE

- Have jaws with fangs that lie parallel to one another and strike forward and down.
- Have four book lungs.
- Are often noticeably hairy.
- While some are small, many can be large bodied (12–75 mm; ½–3 inches).

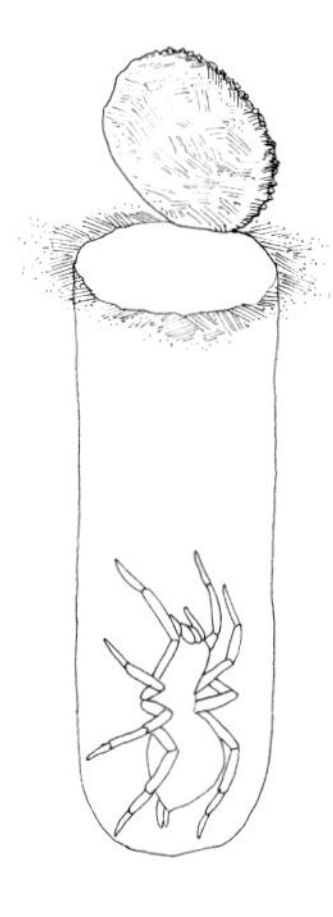

TRAPDOOR SPIDERS (Family *Ctenizidae*)

- Are mainly tropical or subtropical; many species in southern U.S. and some in southern Europe.
- Have a well-camouflaged door that covers their burrow.
- Dig tubelike burrows lined with silk using a spiny rake on their jaws.
- May have posteriorly flattened and hardened abdomen, which can be used to block off the burrow entrance.
- Most are 10–33 MM (⅜–1⅓ inches) long.

FUNNEL-WEB MYGALOMORPHS (Family *Dipluridae*)

- Are mainly tropical; a few species in U.S., Europe, and Australia.
- Large, broad web can be up to 1 meter (1 yard) in diameter.
- Very long spinnerets extend well beyond the abdomen.
- Can be small but some grow up to 50 mm (2 inches).

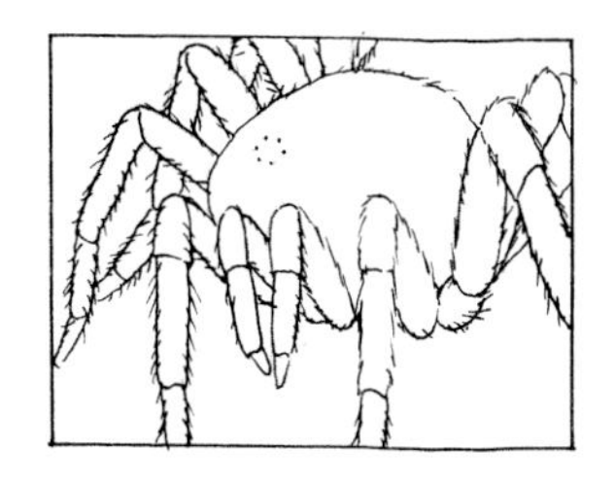

TARANTULAS (Family *Theraphosidae*)

- Are mainly tropical and subtropical; many species in southwestern U.S., none in Europe.
- Live in silk-lined retreats on the ground or in trees or cliff faces.
- Eyes are small and clustered together.
- Are hairy.
- Arboreal species are sometimes called bird-eating spiders.
- Can be small but some many grow up to 50 mm (2 inches).

PURSE-WEB SPIDERS (Family *Atypidae*)

- Are uncommon but widely distributed in North America, Europe, Asia, and Africa.
- Have unusual tubelike web, usually about 200–230 mm (8–9 inches) long; part of the tube lies above ground and is often well camouflaged.
- Are rarely found outside web.
- Have very large jaws.
- Have stout, shiny body.
- Have sharp teeth along basal segment of jaws.

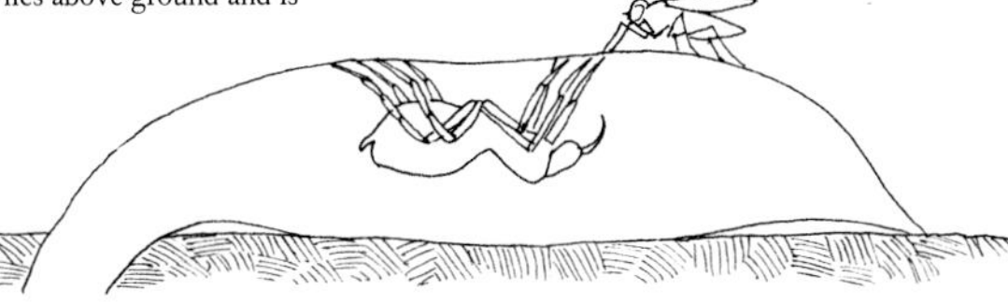

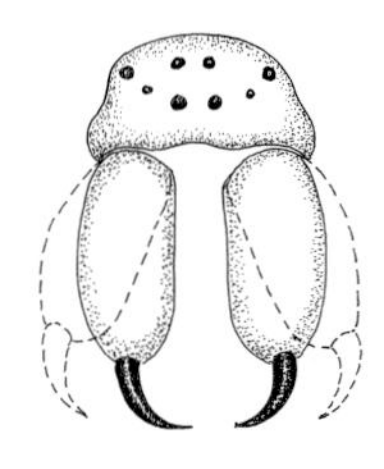

SUBORDER ARANEOMORPHAE

- Have jaws with opposing fangs that move side to side.
- Have two book lungs and/or trachae.
- 90 percent of spiders belong to this suborder.

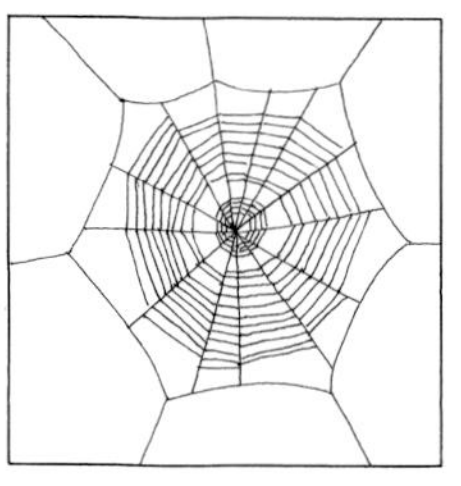

ORB-WEB SPIDERS (Family *Araneidae*)

- Are very common, with worldwide distribution.
- Most spin orb webs, although many structural variations occur between species.
- Webs are usually oriented vertically.

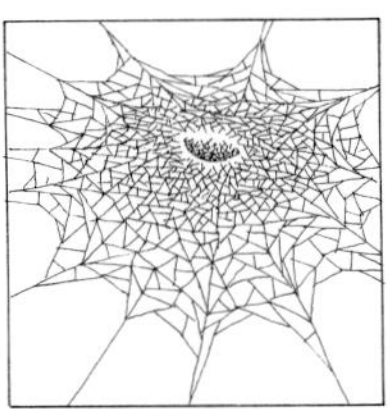

FUNNEL-WEB SPIDERS (Family *Agelenidae*)

- Are common in temperate climates.
- Build small sheet webs with tubular retreat attached; conspicuous webs in lawns.
- Run along top of web.
- Have long, distinctive spinnerets.
- Usually have long and conspicuously hairy legs.
- Also called grass spiders.

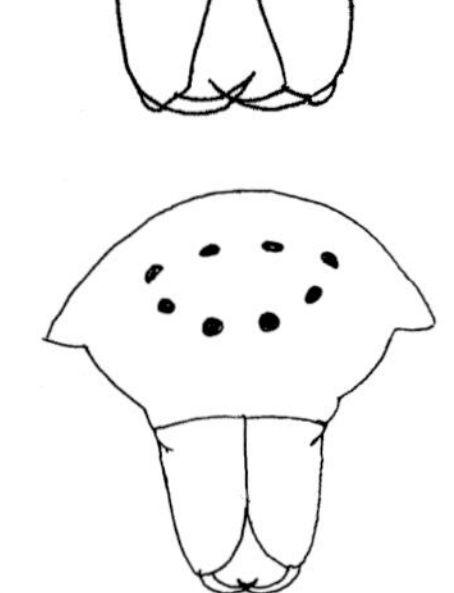

WOLF SPIDERS (Family *Lycosidae*)

- Are very common, with worldwide distribution.
- Free roaming (not associated with a web or permanent shelter); some have silk-lined burrows.
- Are often more active at night.
- Have two noticeably large eyes and six smaller eyes.
- Females attach egg sac to spinnerets and carry young on their backs.
- Are usually gray or brown.

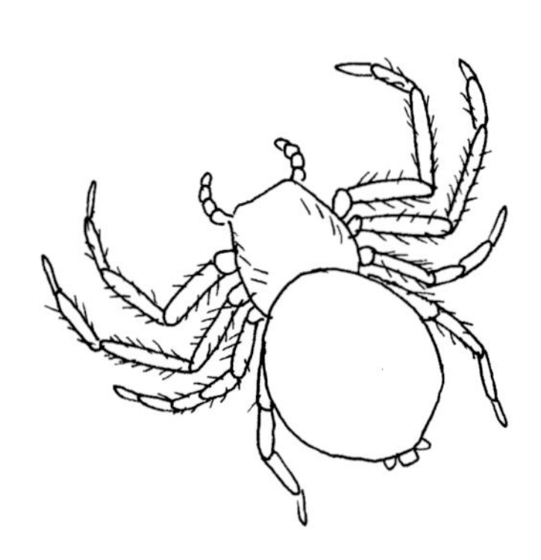

CRAB SPIDERS (Family *Thomisidae*)

- Are very common, with worldwide distribution, especially in tropics and subtropics.
- Do not build a web.
- Are often camouflaged on vegetation.
- Are often brightly colored (pink, yellow, white), although many are drab; some can change color over a period of days.
- Can move forward, backward, and sideways; often slow moving.
- Are crablike in shape and movement; have enlarged front legs and scuttling movements.

JUMPING SPIDERS (Family *Salticidae*)

- Are most diverse in tropics, although abundant in temperate regions.
- Are free living (without permanent shelter).

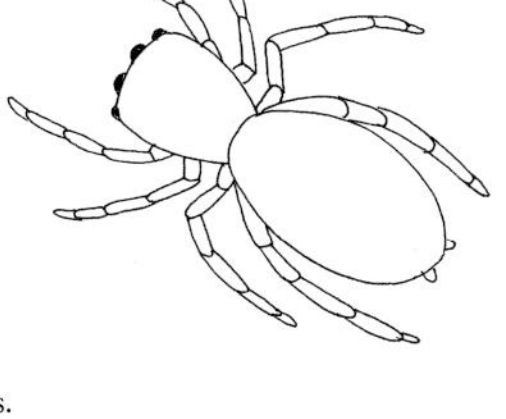

- Are very active during the day and often seen jumping.
- Have large, conspicuous pair of main eyes.
- Are often brightly colored.
- Usually have short, squat bodies with short, powerful legs; some are slender and antlike.
- Are usually small (less than 15 mm [⅝ inch] long).

SIX-EYED SPIDERS (Family *Sicariidae*)

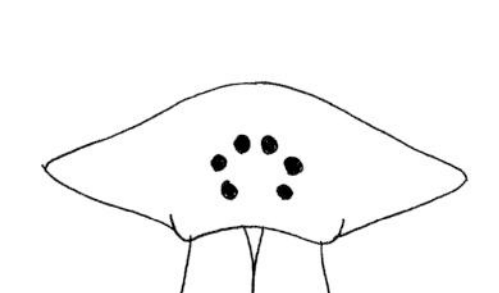

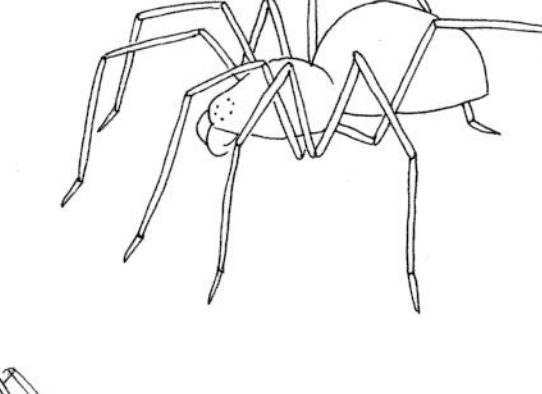

- This is a small family, with about 22 known species (in two genera); mostly occur in the Americas.
- Include the brown recluse spiders and a few close relatives that have venoms known to harm people.
- Have six eyes placed in three pairs.
- Are small to medium size, usually brown, and quite drab.
- Have very thin legs.
- Have untidy web of sticky silk, often seen near human habitation (houses, barns, etc.).

SPITTING SPIDERS (Family *Scytodidae*)

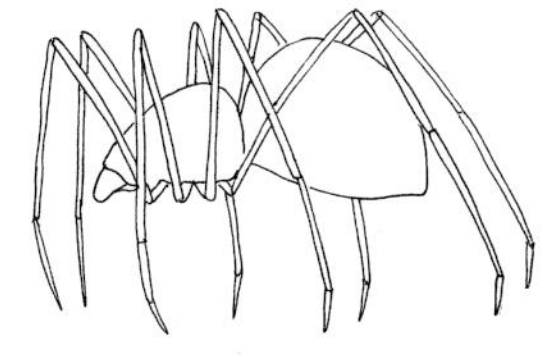

- Most species are tropical or subtropical.
- Do not use a web for prey capture (do use a tangled, random web as a retreat, however); instead spit sticky silk onto prey.
- Have six eyes placed in three pairs.
- Have conspicuous domed carapace.
- Have long, thin legs.

DADDY-LONGLEGS SPIDERS (Family *Pholcidae*)

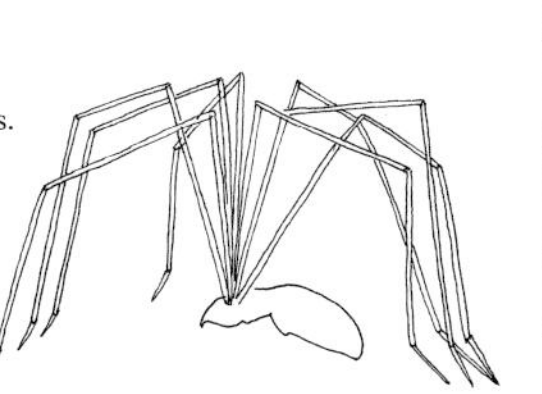

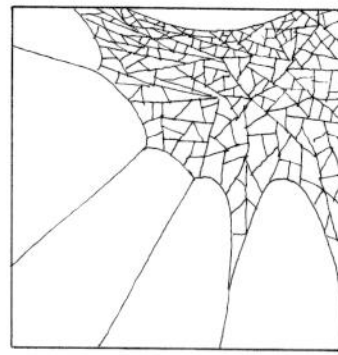

- Have worldwide distribution; some species very common in houses, especially on basement ceilings.
- Also called cellar spiders.
- Have loose, untidy web.
- Are often found hanging upside down in web.
- Have extremely long, thin legs with smallish body.
- Most have eight eyes, although some have six.
- When disturbed, some species bounce vigorously in their webs or on silk threads.

COMB-FOOTED SPIDERS (Family *Theridiidae*)

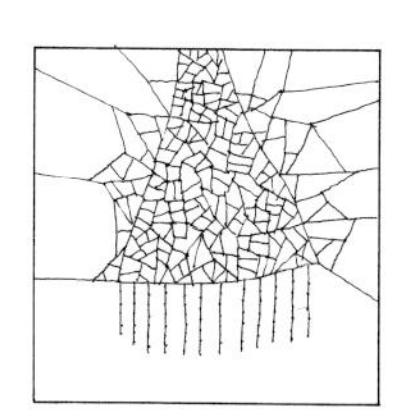

- Are very common, with worldwide distribution.
- Include widow spiders.
- Spin an irregular, tangled cobweb.
- Many have a distinctive globular abdomen.
- Have a narrow row of bristles like a tiny comb on the end of the last pair of legs.

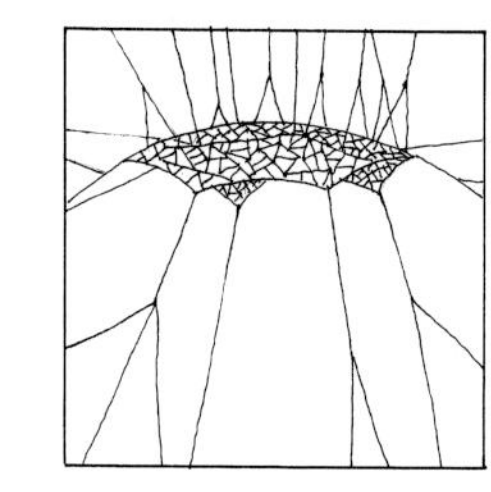

SHEET-WEB SPIDERS (Family *Linyphiidae*)

- This is the largest spider family in temperate climates.
- Are often extremely abundant but usually quite inconspicuous.
- Most are tiny (less than 2 mm [3/32 inch] long).
- Make small sheet web, often domed or sagging slightly (hammock-like).
- Often hang upside down in their webs.
- Are also called dwarf or money spiders.

LONG-JAWED ORB-WEAVERS (Family *Tetragnathidae*)

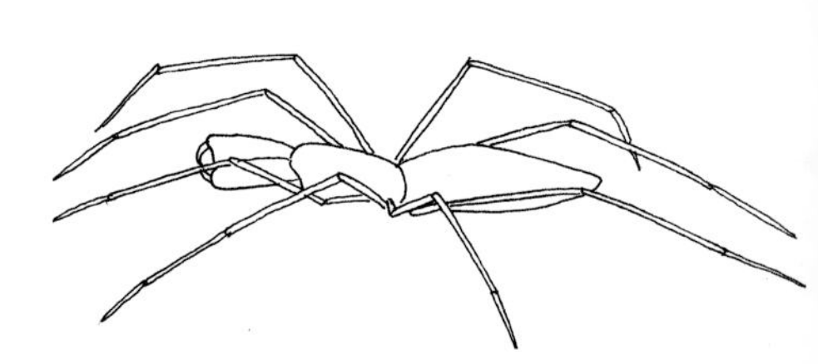

- Most are tropical or subtropical.
- Spin an orb web in which the central part of the hub is often removed (appears as if the web has a hole in the center).
- Webs are usually oriented horizontally or on an angle; rarely vertical.
- Often found near water; sometimes stretch out along blades of grass or other vegetation.
- Often have exceptionally long jaws, especially males.
- Often have long, slim bodies.

NURSERY-WEB SPIDERS (Family *Pisauridae*)

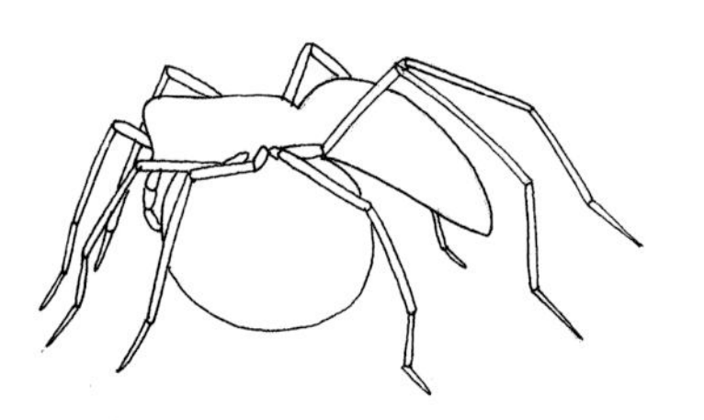

- Have worldwide distribution.
- Are free living.
- Females build tentlike nest (nursery web) for young.
- Resemble wolf spiders but are often much larger (often greater than 15 mm; 5/8 inch).
- Like wolf spiders, have one larger pair of eyes.
- Females carry egg sacs in jaws.
- Include fishing spiders, which can be seen sitting on the water surface.

LYNX SPIDERS (Family *Oxyopidae*)

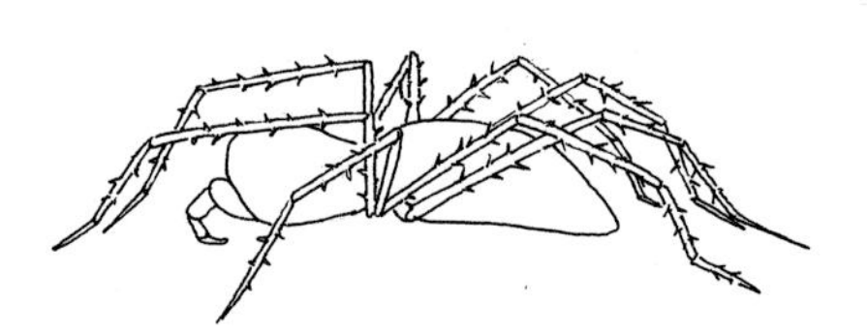

- Most are tropical.
- Are free living.
- Are agile, active spiders.
- Have longish, heavily spined legs.
- Six large eyes form a hexagon, and one smaller pair is situated below them.
- Have slim abdomen that tapers to a point.

INDEX

Page numbers in *italic typeface* type refer to photographs or drawings.